MAXWELL
PLAYS THREE

T0353220

Glyn Maxwell

# PLAYS THREE

ALICE IN WONDERLAND

WIND IN THE WILLOWS

MERLIN AND THE WOODS OF TIME

OBERON BOOKS
LONDON

WWW.OBERONBOOKS.COM

This collection first published in 2017 by Oberon Books Ltd
521 Caledonian Road, London N7 9RH
Tel: +44 (0) 20 7607 3637 / Fax: +44 (0) 20 7607 3629
e-mail: info@oberonbooks.com
www.oberonbooks.com

A catalogue record for this book is available from the British
Library.

PB ISBN: 9781786824028
E ISBN: 9781786824035

Cover design: Konstantinos Vasdekis

# Contents

## Open Air and House of Stories

*Once in the woods of a world you know*
*A story grew where the lime-trees grow*

One day in the spring of 2011, I received a call from my friend the director Alex Clifton, asking me if I'd write a play for a summer season in his native city of Chester. Assuming he wanted this play for the summer of 2012, I said yes okay why not, and by the time I realized it was needed in a matter of weeks for the summer that was coming, I was too intrigued to change my mind. He also said the play could be 'about anything', which he then slightly modified to 'as long as it's about Robin Hood or Camelot'.

In a month or so I wrote *Merlin and the Woods Of Time,* and thus began a very fruitful relationship with the city of Chester, with English classics, with Alex as both director and cultural pioneer, with the city's Open-Air Theatre in Grosvenor Park, and, since May 2017, with its beautiful, brand-new, cultural centre: Storyhouse.

The three plays collected here, *Alice in Wonderland, Wind in the Willows* and the *Merlin* play, along with three others – *The Beggar's Opera, Cyrano De Bergerac,* and *Masters Are You Mad?* (a sequel for *Twelfth Night*) – were all written specially for the Open-Air Theatre or for Storyhouse. All six plays are more or less adaptations of classics, five English, one French, and (with the exception of *The Beggar's Opera,* an adult show designed for the thrust stage at Storyhouse) all were written to be played in the round, indoors or out, in rain or shine, to pretty much all ages.

I've been at home with outdoor theatre since childhood, when I watched Death come to Everyman in the grounds of a German castle. I saw Shakespeare done in various parks to various standards and by the early 1990s was staging my own first plays in my parents' Hertfordshire garden. So the fresh air at Chester was a welcome gift to both life and work. Something about the changing sky, the wind in the trees, church bells, the whims of the weather-gods, gives me a sense of openness, honesty, community, equality – an age-old feeling, augmented for me on both a historical level, Chester being an ancient home of English theatre with its great cycle of Mystery Plays, and a personal one, my parents having hailed from the Wirral and nearby Flintshire.

Alice, the Hatter, the Red Queen, Mole and Ratty and Toad, Lancelot and Guinevere, Cyrano and Roxanne, Macheath, Polly Peachum, Olivia, Malvolio – what writer wouldn't want to sound these immortal voices again? But to sound them in the rhythms of Now under a Cheshire sky is to sound England at this moment, because language cannot help but speak the news. And whether it's Alice finding adulthood to be a sphere of nonsense, poor Mole no longer knowing where her home is in the forest, or the humble servant Watercup trapped in the farcical madness of Camelot, these are plays of the open-hearted treading on through flickering, threatening shadows. Like all new drama, they're the news by other means.

The very first lines of the first of these plays, quoted above, were written for Grosvenor Park and its lime trees, and sung to an audience of 200 or so picnickers in July 2011. The season was brief, the conditions only adequate, the actors got changed in a shed across the road. But *something* was growing: the audience, year on year, from 5000 to 27,000 theatregoers in six seasons. By 2017 that charming picnic venue had become a 600-seater theatre-in-the-round, the largest professional open-air space outside London, playing three shows in repertory throughout the summer. And in May 2017, largely on the back of this success, driven by Alex as Artistic Director and Andrew Bentley as Chief Executive Officer, Chester opened its brand-new Storyhouse, the city's first indoor theatre since the closure of the Gateway in 2007. The audience for the first Storyhouse season was 43,000.

Storyhouse is a story in itself. To walk into this magnificent cultural centre – which combines a library, a cinema, a restaurant, a black-box studio, and a state-of-the-art 500-seat theatre that transforms to a grand 800-seater when required, almost entirely *council*-funded, with radically egalitarian and progressive policies on inclusion and pricing, gender-fairness and diversity as absolute principles, and a remarkable community ethic – is to stumble into a very bright sunlit place at a darkening time for the arts and culture and civic – even *civil* – discourse in this country.

For in that sunlit place one finds both the soul of a country and the beating heart of theatre: one finds there every kind of person, of every stripe and generation, the hopeful and fearful, the knowing and unknowing, those at war with their times, those at peace with time itself. And their conflicts and collisions make history, make theatre, whether they end in cheer and confetti, or tears and redemption, or dry wisdom in the ruins. No matter where the story's going, every voice is welcome, for light or for dark or for the dance of that old duo, every voice will be heard there before the sun goes down.

It is a continuing honour and delight to have contributed my plays to this inspiring and still unfolding work.

**Glyn Maxwell, November 2017**

ALICE IN WONDERLAND

adapted from the books *Alice's Adventures In Wonderland*
and *Through The Looking-Glass* by Lewis Carroll

*for Alfie*

# Dramatis Personae

ALICE,

and ALICIA, the SAME GIRL;

MARY, HER NANNY,

ALICE'S MOTHER,

A DOCTOR;

A WHITE RABBIT;

TIGER-LILY,

VIOLET,

ROSE, THE LIVE FLOWERS;

A CATERPILLAR,

A DESK,

HUMPTY-DUMPTY,

1ST KING'S MAN,

2ND KING'S MAN,

3RD KING'S MAN,

A DUCHESS,

A DODO,

A CHESHIRE CAT,

A HATTER,

A MARCH HARE,

A DORMOUSE,

PAWN 2,

PAWN 5,

PAWN 7,

A RED KING,

A LION,

A UNICORN,

TWEEDLEDUM AND

TWEEDLEDEE

*Alice in Wonderland* was the second play performed in the opening season of the Storyhouse Theatre in Chester. It opened on 19 May 2017, and later transferred to the Open Air Theatre in the same city. The play was staged in repertory with *The Beggar's Opera,* also by Glyn Maxwell.

*Cast*
Rebecca Birch – ALICE
Tom Connor – WHITE RABBIT, MARCH HARE
Jonathan Dryden Taylor – CATERPILLAR, RED KING, DOCTOR
Daniel Goode – HUMPTY DUMPTY, PAWN 7, LION
Charlotte Gorton – DUCHESS, MOTHER
Barbara Hockaday – MARY, ROSE
Anna Leong Brophy – ALICIA
Charlotte Miranda Smith – VIOLET, PAWN 5
Caolan McCarthy – CHESHIRE CAT, TWEEDLEDUM, PAWN 2
Alex Mugnaioni – HATTER, UNICORN
Baker Mukasa – ALICE'S DESK, DORMOUSE, TWEEDLEDEE
Nancy Sullivan – TIGER LILY

*Creative Team*
Derek Bond – Director
Jessica Curtis – Designer
Rob Halliday – Lighting Designer
Jude Obermüller – Composer
Kay Magson – Casting

*Stage Management Team*
Helen Keast – Company Stage Manager
Natalie James-Fox – Stage Manager
Suzie Foster – DSM
Roberta Gleaves – ASM
Evie Oliver – ASM
Antonella Petraccaro – Costume Supervisor
Therese Denis – Wardrobe Supervisor

*For Chester Performs*
Andrew Bentley – Chief Executive Officer
Alex Clifton – Artistic Director

# ACT ONE

## 1 – THE PICNIC

*ALICIA and her nanny MARY arrive with picnic things on a sunny late August afternoon in a meadow*

ALICIA:       How can you have a picnic with one person?

MARY:         There are two of us, dear.

ALICIA:       I mean only one *child*, Mary, I have no one to play with, no one to talk to, I probably never will have again.

MARY:         Oh what nonsense you talk!

ALICIA:       Lory has swanned off to school to be Head Girl or Class Queen or something, and Edie can go on playing games in the prep-school for *ever*, it's only me to who the bad things happen!

MARY:         Me to *whom*, me to *whom*...

ALICIA:       But it isn't you it's me!

MARY:         Come now, Alicia, Lory's told you all about it, it's a very smart school you're going to, your mother's so proud.

ALICIA:       It's all right for *Lory*, she loves it, she's Empress of All Prefects or something, and stop calling me Alicia, I'm *Alice*.

MARY:         Yes you've always been Alice because you couldn't say 'Alicia' as a child, but you *can* say it now, you're a young lady now, won't you try a vol-au-vent?

ALICIA:       I *won't* try a vovolong and I'm *not* a young lady, I'm Alice and I want some cake!

MARY:         Well it isn't time for cake yet, there'll be time enough later.

| | |
|---|---|
| ALICIA: | Some picnic... |
| MARY: | Oh come now. |
| ALICIA: | Because it *looks* like all the lovely days of summer, and it *sounds* like them and *smells* like them but it isn't, you know, it's a traitor, it's not one of them at all, because it knows it's the very last, it knows it's the last one *ever!* |
| MARY: | Oh Alicia... |
| ALICIA: | And you can hear the river running, it's saying *nothing ever stops, Alice, everything must change, Alice, clouds come, the sun goes down!* so tomorrow I have to wear a horrid black uniform and take the train to boring-school – |
| MARY: | *Boarding*-school! |
| ALICIA: | Where I won't have mummy or Edie, or you even, and the teachers will scream at me, and I won't know any answers, I'll be lost in the corridors and make no friends, Lory said, Lory *said*, she was cackling she was, she said there's *nothing worse to be* than a new girl at the start of term! |
| MARY: | Oh she was teasing... |
| ALICIA: | And at the end of the day, she says there's a Great Big Bully who comes looking for the new girls – |
| MARY: | Alicia *stop!* |
| ALICIA: | I'm Alice! – What's in that bottle? |

*ALICE has noticed MARY sipping discreetly from a hipflask*

| | |
|---|---|
| MARY: | It's only my cordial. |
| ALICIA: | *I* want some cordial. |
| MARY: | When you're older. |
| ALICIA: | I don't *want* to be older. |

| | |
|---|---|
| MARY: | Don't you want to grow up and know everything about everything? |
| ALICIA: | Yes. One day. |
| MARY: | Then you have to go to school, Alicia. |
| ALICIA: | Very well. I'll go to school as Alicia, and do all the things I have to as Alicia, but I'll stay behind as Alice, and do all the things *she* wants to! |
| MARY: | And how do you think you'll achieve both things? |
| ALICIA: | Not telling. |

*ALICIA clasps her hands together and closes her eyes*

| | |
|---|---|
| MARY: | Suit yourself. What are you doing? |
| ALICIA: | Not telling. |
| MARY: | That's a shame. |
| ALICIA: | Because it's magic. |
| MARY: | Oh I see… |
| ALICIA: | So it's a secret. |
| MARY: | Right you are. |
| ALICIA: | So you can't tell anyone. |
| MARY: | Cross my heart. |
| ALICIA: | It's a spell which I've perfected. |
| MARY: | Perfected it, have you, what's it a spell for? |
| ALICIA: | It's not a spell *for*, it's a spell *against*, a spell against Time, and if it works I won't have to go to boring-school tomorrow and meet the teachers or the Bully. |
| MARY: | Right you are. |
| ALICIA: | It slows Time down, it was perfected at the sundial by Edie and me, it always worked until today, but if you clasp it tight enough it makes Time stop completely, then you can do anything you like! |

| | |
|---|---|
| MARY: | Right you are. |
| ALICIA: | Mary? |
| MARY: | Right you are. |
| ALICIA: | Mary? |

*The spell worked. ALICIA checks that time has stopped for MARY*

| | |
|---|---|
| ALICIA: | Ha! I'm not going to boring-school now, Mary. |
| MARY: | Right you are. |
| ALICIA: | I'm staying at the prep-school, in fact I'm going to stay at home because the Queen has decreed another whole month of summer holidays! |

*Suddenly there are two of them*

| | |
|---|---|
| ALICE: | No she hasn't. |
| ALICIA: | Pardon? |
| ALICE: | It's a whole *year* of summer holidays. |
| ALICIA: | A whole year? |
| ALICE: | A whole *life* of summer holidays. The Queen said so. |
| ALICIA: | I didn't know that. |
| ALICE: | You do now. |

*ALICIA and ALICE contemplate each other*

| | |
|---|---|
| ALICIA/ALICE: | I like your hair. I like yours too. I like your dress. Yours is nice. What's your name. You first. I'm Alice. |
| ALICIA: | *I'm* – actually I'm *Alicia*. It's like Alice but more elegant. |
| ALICE: | No it's not, shall we play? |
| ALICIA: | If you like. No one's watching. |
| ALICE/ALICIA: | Best friends? Best friends forever! What's your favourite game? Hide and Seek. Hide and Seek! |

| | |
|---|---|
| ALICIA: | But we're not enough people for Hide and Seek. |
| ALICE: | Yes we are! I'll hide, you seek! |
| ALICIA: | But when I find you I've won and then it's over. |
| ALICE: | But if you don't find me *I've* won and then it's over. |
| ALICIA: | But I'd keep on seeking so it wouldn't be over. |
| ALICE: | And I'd keep on hiding and you'd seek me forever. |
| ALICIA: | But if I never found you we'd never meet again. |
| ALICE: | I suppose, I'd still be the winner though. |
| ALICIA: | Yes but I'd be sad. |
| ALICE: | Because I won? yes you would be. |
| ALICIA: | No, that's not why. |
| ALICE: | I'd be happy being the winner! |
| ALICIA: | You'd be lonely though if no one ever found you. |
| ALICE: | No I wouldn't. There'd be all sorts of creatures hiding there and we'd all have won the game. |
| ALICIA: | I think you'd all have lost the game. At any rate, I know why you're here. There are *two* of us now, so I can achieve both things, I can go to boring-school tomorrow and I can learn everything about everything, and at the same time I can stay here and play, because I'll be *you*, dear, and all will be just exactly like I said it should be. I have my cake *and* eat it, do you understand? |
| ALICE: | Look a butterfly… |

ALICIA:        I'm trying to explain, you know. You're
to stay here and play in the meadow,
while Mary sits there, and you can run off
anywhere you like, because she'll stay just
like that and the afternoon will ever end –

ALICE:        Look a White Rabbit.

*A WHITE RABBIT hurries through, checking her watch*

ALICE:        Why are you checking your watch, White
Rabbit, don't you know there's no Time?

ALICIA:        Come now, rabbits don't check their
watches.

ALICE:        Yes they're usually too busy.

ALICIA:        No Alice, they don't because they're rabbits.

ALICE:        He was, Leesha, he was checking his watch,
then he went down the rabbit-hole!

ALICIA:        It's *Alicia*, and he might do that in a fiction,
you know, but fictions are in books. You're
*me*, you know, Alice, you see what I see!

ALICE:        I'm *not* you, I'm Alice, and you're obviously
blind.

ALICIA:        You're evidently mad.

ALICE:        You're the worst friend ever.

ALICIA:        You're the worst *person* ever.

ALICE:        You're a pig!

ALICIA:        You're a pig and no returns.

ALICE:        You're a witch and I say *barley!*

ALICIA:        I say *fainites!*

ALICE/ALICIA:    *Infinity!*

*They cross their fingers against each other*

ALICE:        Wait for me, White Rabbit! Wait for me, best
friend! I'm stuck with boring grown-up Leesha!

*ALICE runs off after the WHITE RABBIT*

ALICIA:        Good luck making friends with rabbits, ha!
What a silly little girl she is. She's impossible
– it's *all* impossible – Mary? Mary I don't –
I don't feel quite myself...

*Now they've parted, the spell is broken. MARY wakes up, in time to see
that ALICIA is unwell, swaying – MARY catches her as she falls, and
hurries her off home...*

## 2 – ALICE IN WONDERLAND

*Strange Creatures, Wonders*

ALICE:        Well, after seeing this I shall think nothing
of a haunted house. How brave they'll think
me at home... Mary? She can't hear me
now. Leesha? I don't need *her* help. I wonder
where I've come to. I must be getting
somewhere near the centre of the earth...
oh what nonsense I'm talking! Where has
everyone gone? Which way to go now?
Which way?

*A strange gate appears and opens*

ALICE:        Curiouser and curiouser... It must be –
it must be *tomorrow*, this must be boring-
school! But it's really not *that* boring...

*The WHITE RABBIT runs through*

ALICE:        White Rabbit!

W RABBIT:    Oh dear, oh dear, I shall be late, I shall be
late!

ALICE:        Stop, White Rabbit, stop, I need to ask you
something, I'm a new girl!

W RABBIT:    No time, no time! Oh my ears and whiskers,
how late it's getting, how late!

ALICE:        It isn't late it's early! *I'm* early, look!

W RABBIT:    What's that? You can't be early when it's
late!

| | |
|---|---|
| ALICE: | Oh but I am, I came early, to make a good impression. |
| W RABBIT: | A good impression of what? |
| ALICE: | I said – a new girl. |
| W RABBIT: | May I see your impression of a new girl? |
| ALICE: | Pardon? I don't understand. I'm looking for my classroom. |
| W RABBIT: | Hmm yes that's very good, bravo! Very convincing. |
| ALICE: | Oh. Thank you, well, my mummy said I should make a good impression by being early. So it's not late at all and you shouldn't be so worried. |
| W RABBIT: | But the Queen, the Queen, I'm keeping her waiting! |

*The WHITE RABBIT hurries away*

| | |
|---|---|
| ALICE: | The *Queen* goes to this school? Well Mary said it was a smart school. Was that yesterday? I – don't remember travelling here, there must have been a train, and look at me – I don't have the black uniform. Oh no! I'll stand out! I'll be the only one! What if the Bully comes, I need to hide, I need to hide! Too late! |

*LIVE FLOWERS come, TIGER-LILY, VIOLET and ROSE, colourful but nonetheless in black uniform. They see ALICE in her blue dress*

| | |
|---|---|
| TIGER-LILY: | Ha, look at *her*, she hasn't got her uniform. |
| VIOLET: | Yeah look at *her*, standing out like that. |
| ROSE: | *And* she's the only one! |
| ALICE: | I'm new! I'm the new girl! |
| TIGER-LILY: | If she had the right clothes she would fit in very well. |

| | |
|---|---|
| VIOLET: | If she had the right look she would look just right. |
| ROSE: | If she was like one of us she'd be just like one of us! |
| TIGER-LILY: | You're in trouble now New Girl! It's the Caterpillar! |
| VIOLET:/ROSE: | The Caterpillar! |

*The cackle and hurry away*

| | |
|---|---|
| ALICE: | I'm trying my best! But I don't have a uniform – where do I find my uniform? |

*A CATERPILLAR comes, smoking a shisha*

| | |
|---|---|
| CATERPILLAR: | In your desk, of course. |
| ALICE: | But – where do I find my desk? |
| CATERPILLAR: | That all depends who you are. Who are you? |
| ALICE: | I – *[she coughs in the smoke]* – I hardly know, Mr, um, Caterpillar sir, just now, I mean, I knew who I was yesterday, I was with my nanny Mary by the river, but now yesterday's gone – |
| CATERPILLAR: | And where *is* Yesterday? |
| ALICE: | I – I don't know *[she coughs again]* it's gone up in smoke! |
| CATERPILLAR: | Wrong from beginning to end. You mean you've lost it, don't you. |
| ALICE: | Pardon? No! |
| CATERPILLAR: | Or perhaps the cat ate it. |
| ALICE: | No, Dinah would never do that! |
| CATERPILLAR: | So where did you last *see* Yesterday? |
| ALICE: | Well, I saw it last night, I suppose – |
| CATERPILLAR: | And where did you put it? |
| ALICE: | Where did I – put it? |

| | |
|---|---|
| CATERPILLAR: | Where did you *put* Yesterday, silly girl, it's probably in your desk, isn't it, along with your uniform. |
| ALICE: | I don't see how that's silly, sir, because nobody told me where my desk was, so I didn't – |
| CATERPILLAR: | Oh I see, and you just do what Nobody tells you, do you? |
| ALICE: | Pardon? I don't understand! This isn't fair! I want to go home! |
| CATERPILLAR: | You should keep your head, you know. |
| ALICE: | There's nothing wrong with my head! |
| CATERPILLAR: | You just lost it, it's probably in your desk. |
| ALICE: | But where *is* my desk? |
| CATERPILLAR: | That all depends who you are. Who are you? |
| ALICE: | I'm Alice, Alice, *ALICE!!!* |
| CATERPILLAR: | Call the register! |
| DESKS: | **CALL THE REGISTER!** |

*EMPTY DESKS rush in and make an empty classroom*

| | |
|---|---|
| ALICE: | But – where is everyone? And which desk is mine? My name is Alice, so I normally come first… |

*She nervously sits at the first desk*

| | |
|---|---|
| CATERPILLAR: | **ABIGAIL!** |
| ALICE: | Oh in this class I come second… |

*ALICE moves to the next*

| | |
|---|---|
| CATERPILLAR: | **ADELE!** |
| ALICE: | Oh perhaps I'm third… |

*ALICE moves to the next*

| | |
|---|---|
| CATERPILLAR: | **ADRIANA…** |

*ALICE keeps moving down the desks*

| | |
|---|---|
| CATERPILLAR: | ALANA, ALANIS, ALFREDA, ALFRESCO, ALGEBRA, ALGORITHM, ALIBI… |
| ALICE: | *Alibi?* this is nonsense! |
| CATERPILLAR: | …and ALICE. |

*ALICE reaches the very last DESK and sits there relieved and exhausted*

| | |
|---|---|
| ALICE: | Sir, nobody's here. |
| CATERPILLAR: | Let me mark that down: *Nobody is present,* thank you, Nobody, *so* nice of you to show up. |
| ALICE: | I'm not Nobody I'm Somebody, I'm Alice, I have a desk and it says ALICE! |
| DESK: | Alice. |
| ALICE: | Thank you, Desk. Finally! |
| CATERPILLAR: | Now take out your completed homework ready to hand in when I come back. That's the end of this period. Now I have to change. |

*The CATERPILLAR leaves, as do all the other DESKS*

| | |
|---|---|
| ALICE: | Homework? No! It's my first day! I'm new! I don't know anything! I wasn't here before! What was the homework? |
| DESK: | Search me. |
| ALICE: | I *am* searching you, Desk, but I can't find anything! |
| DESK: | *[Sing-song.]* You ain't done yer homework. |
| ALICE: | There wasn't any homework, Desk! I was at home, I don't *work* at home, I play there! |
| DESK: | Ooh we don't play *here*, you're in deep trouble. |
| ALICE: | It's not fair! |
| DESK: | *He* didn't do his homework, and he'll be payin' the price. |

| | |
|---|---|
| ALICE: | He? Who's he? |
| DESK: | Oi, Dumpty, get yourself over here! New girl. |
| ALICE: | Dumpty? As in *Humpty*-Dumpty? |

*HUMPTY-DUMPTY appears, very pleased with himself*

| | |
|---|---|
| CHORUS: | *In winter when the fields are white* |
| | *He sings this song for your delight* |
| | *In spring when woods throw off their green* |
| | *He'll try and tell you what he means!* |
| | *In summer when the days are long* |
| | *Perhaps you'll understand the song* |
| | *In autumn when the leaves are brown* |
| | *Take pen and ink and write it down!* |
| ALICE: | (He really is quite like an egg.) |
| HUMPTY: | It's very provoking to be called an egg, very! |
| ALICE: | Oh I'm sorry. The Desk says you haven't done your homework, Mr Dumpty. |
| HUMPTY: | I am one of the Gloucestershire Dumpties and I do not *do* homework. I am *always* top of my class. |
| ALICE: | Are you? Mr and Mrs – Dumpty must be very proud. |
| HUMPTY: | *Doctor* and Mrs Dumpty. |
| ALICE: | Oh I'm sorry, (I feel like I'm treading on eggshells) |
| HUMPTY: | What? |
| ALICE: | I mean, sorry, so, your, your father's a doctor? That might be quite useful, I mean, in the, the near future. |
| HUMPTY: | Why? |
| ALICE: | Oh – no reason. My father's a dean. |
| HUMPTY: | I do declare. |
| ALICE: | It's very nice to meet you, Mr Dumpty, *my* name is Alice. |

| | |
|---|---|
| HUMPTY: | That's a stupid name. What does it mean? |
| ALICE: | Oh, it – well – must it mean something? |
| HUMPTY: | Of course it must. *My* name means the shape I am, and it's a good, handsome shape isn't it? My brothers, Kenneth Dumpty and Nigel Dumpty, they look nothing like me. But with a name like yours, what is it, |
| ALICE: | Alice. |
| HUMPTY: | You might be any shape at all, star-shape, spiral, oblong. |
| ALICE: | But I'm this shape, and where I come from, names don't have to *mean* things – |
| HUMPTY: | Well we're not where you come from, we're where *I* come from, and when *I* use a word, it means just what I choose it to mean, neither more nor less. |
| ALICE: | I see. |
| HUMPTY: | Yes, you do. |
| ALICE: | I – I was wondering what was the homework you didn't do, Mr Dumpty? |
| HUMPTY: | Oh some ridiculous poem or other. I was told to memorize it. The Gloucestershire Dumpties do not memorize poems, I know all about poems, I passed Poetry. |
| ALICE: | Can one *pass* Poetry? |
| HUMPTY: | *One* can do as he pleases, but *I* passed it with distinction. I can explain all the poems that were ever invented, and a good many that haven't been invented yet. |
| ALICE: | I say. |
| HUMPTY: | Yes, you do. |
| ALICE: | But you haven't done the homework? |

HUMPTY: Oh, the teachers tried to get me interested, they said the poem was all about me! I said thank you I'm flattered, but I've other fish to fry.

ALICE: Does the poem in question begin with your name?

HUMPTY: *Obviously.* All poems *ought* to begin with my name. All sheets of paper do, once I get my hands on 'em.

ALICE: But you didn't memorize it.

HUMPTY: I didn't even read it. I can imagine how it goes so I don't need to.

ALICE: How do you think it goes?

HUMPTY: Well, my guess would be, if it tells it like it is, it would go something like *Humpty-Dumpty, top of the class, he rose to glory,*

ALICE: He fell on his –

HUMPTY: I detest rhyme, it's so reductive. I am now weary of passing time with you, New Girl, so I shall go and sit on that high narrow wall over there and pass the time of day.

ALICE: But, but, Mr Dumpty, it's really not a long poem, I think it would do you good to read it, you know, it might help you to make the right choices in life. That's a very *high* wall –

HUMPTY: The Gloucestershire Dumpties do not make the right choices in life, and we've been around for several centuries. In fact we've been *extremely* round for several centuries. Goodbye.

ALICE: Yes. Be careful, won't you? Then we'll meet again!

HUMPTY: I shouldn't know you again if we *did* meet, you're exactly like everyone else.

*HUMPTY goes*

| | |
|---|---|
| ALICE: | Of all the unsatisfactory people I ever met… How can he get away with never doing his homework? |

*The WHITE RABBIT runs through*

| | |
|---|---|
| ALICE: | White Rabbit, come back! |
| W RABBIT: | I'm late, I'm late, no time to lose! |
| ALICE: | *I* have some time, Rabbit, you can borrow some from me! (I think I'm getting the hang of this school.) |
| W RABBIT: | Oh dear, well, it's quite irregular, but if it's going spare… |
| ALICE: | It is, and I wanted to ask you some questions. |
| W RABBIT: | Oh dearie me, my ears and whiskers… |
| ALICE: | Who is the Queen here, where do I find her, where do I go for lunch, where can I find a friend, who's the Great Big Bully who comes at the end of the day and is she really so bad? my mummy says bullies are little frightened people, but – well, start with the Queen, who *is* this Queen? |
| W RABBIT: | Oh dear, oh my, the *Red* Queen of course, she'll be *savage* if I keep her waiting any longer! |
| ALICE: | You can blame me, Rabbit. |
| W RABBIT: | Then you'll lose your head for sure! |
| ALICE: | What do you mean by that? |
| W RABBIT: | Just what I say! Or the *White* Queen, oh my… |
| ALICE: | Who's the White Queen? |
| W RABBIT: | She's even worse! |
| ALICE: | But you said the Red Queen was *savage*, how can the White Queen be worse than savage? Nothing's worse than savage. |

| W RABBIT: | She… she… |

*The WHITE RABBIT lowers his voice – and himself towards the ground, bringing ALICE down with him – to whisper this*

| W RABBIT: | She… *doesn't – believe in us.* |
| ALICE: | Oh. Well she'll believe in me all right, because look: I'm right here! |
| W RABBIT: | *She doesn't – believe – in anything.* Huh! I've said too much, it's too late, I'm late, I'll always be late! |

*The WHITE RABBIT flees in terror. From off, a roar and a mighty crash as HUMPTY falls off his wall. Three of the KING'S MEN come through*

| 1st MAN | Code-red, team, we have a code-red! Where the devil are those horses? |
| 2nd MAN | D'you reckon we'll be able to put him together again? |
| 1st MAN | I very much doubt it. |
| 3rd MAN | We ain't got time for this, lads, we're overstretched as it is! |
| 2nd MAN | Sittin' on a wall, for pete's sake. Dumpty you *numpty.* |

*They go*

| ALICE: | *I* know that poem off by heart, *I'm* not in trouble at all! And those two Queens just sound silly. If you were savage you wouldn't have any friends. And if you didn't believe in anything you wouldn't even believe in yourself and what a pickle you'd be in then! Oh, it seems I am a little hungry. |
| DESK: | So eat your packed lunch. |

*The DESK hands ALICE a box*

| ALICE: | This certainly wasn't here before. |
| DESK: | You weren't hungry before. |

| | |
|---|---|
| ALICE: | What a very curious Desk you are. |
| DESK: | I ain't curious at all. I don't ask questions. I'm open to ideas, but I shut it when I have to. That's a riddle, innit. |
| ALICE: | Is the answer – *desk?* |
| DESK: | Oh wot! I can't *believe* she solved that so quick. Here's another riddle: why am I like a raven? |
| ALICE: | Do shut up, Desk. – Now, DRINK ME, it says on this bottle. And EAT ME, on this tin. There's a cake inside, ooh, icing too… |

*ALICE eats*

| | |
|---|---|
| ALICE: | Hmm, oo, yes, this is – *AMAZING*, it's the best cake I've ever – I want more, I need more, I *deserve* more, yes, yes! Look, there's less than there was – soon it will all be gone! More! More cake! Somebody bring more cake! Dinner ladies! I know my way round school now, I'm not new any more, people look up to me, I'm going to be Head Girl like Lory! Now I'll have the drink too, it's probably even better! |

*ALICE drinks*

| | |
|---|---|
| ALICE: | There! That's – really not very – hm. I feel rather silly now, having eaten so much cake. I feel rather a fool. People will laugh at me. If *I* were me *I* would. What a ridiculous thing to say. Now I feel ridiculous *and* silly. I wish that other girl Leesha had come with me. *She* would have made friends by now, *she* would have done her homework. Maybe she would have looked after me. No one's looking after me, no one sees me, perhaps I'll just – go out, like a candle. At least I won't get into trouble. And I do have a friend right here, |

I have my Desk. You're my friend, aren't you, Desk? Desk?

*The DESK runs away as the FLOWERS come back: TIGER-LILY, VIOLET and ROSE*

TIGER-LILY: I say, was New Girl talking to her desk?

VIOLET: That's because she's got no friends.

ROSE: That's because she's not like us.

VIOLET: She's probably just like *her.*

TIGER-LILY: *Typical* of her to be just like her.

ALICE: Excuse me, um, Flowers, do you think I might have a talk with you?

TIGER-LILY: We *would* talk with you, if you had anything worth saying.

ALICE: I do, I do, I think *everything's* worth saying!

VIOLET: Go on then.

ALICE: Pardon? How do you mean?

VIOLET: You think everything's worth saying, so say everything.

TIGER-LILY: We're waiting, New Girl.

ROSE: How thrilling, is she going to say *everything?* I've never heard everything.

ALICE: I can't – say *everything.*

TIGER-LILY: You can't say *anything,* what kind of a flower *are* you?

ALICE: I'm – not a flower, I'm a girl, and where *I* come from, flowers don't talk.

VIOLET: Don't talk?

ALICE: Not a word.

TIGER-LILY: What on *earth* do they do?

ALICE: Well, they just – grow.

TIGER-LILY: Oh how vulgar.

| | |
|---|---|
| VIOLET: | Barbaric. |
| ROSE: | *Poor* flowers… |
| TIGER-LILY: | And how do they know *how* to grow? |
| VIOLET: | Yeah, who taught them that? |
| ALICE: | I – don't know. That's a funny question. |
| TIGER-LILY: | So why aren't you laughing? If you want to be our friend, New Girl, you should laugh each time we're funny. |
| ALICE: | Very well, I'll try to. |
| TIGER-LILY: | Have you done your homework yet? |
| ALICE: | Yes, yes, it's, wait, *Humpty-Dumpty sat on a wall –* |
| VIOLET: | That's not your homework, that's current events. |
| ALICE: | Ha ha, that's very good… |
| VIOLET: | What are you laughing at? That wasn't funny. |
| ALICE: | I'm sorry, it sounded funny. |
| VIOLET: | Nothing about current events is funny. |
| ALICE: | I'll try to remember. |
| ROSE: | Why don't you have any friends? |
| ALICE: | I did, I did have a friend called Leesha, in the meadow, but I left her behind, and she isn't really my friend, she's actually quite bossy, she's more like a sister, but she's not a sister either, she's sort of like a cross between a sister and a – |
| TIGER-LILY: | I can see why she's got no friends, she doesn't half bang on. |
| VIOLET: | Yeah and she laughs at current events. |
| ROSE: | Has she said everything yet? |
| ALICE: | Please! I'm just – trying to make friends. |

| | |
|---|---|
| TIGER-LILY: | *Make* friends? You can't just *make* friends, New Girl, out of papier-mâché. We three go back, we have history. |
| VIOLET: | We do, we met in the nursery garden. |
| ROSE: | On the golden afternoon, ah… |
| TIGER-LILY: | Where were *you?* is the question. |
| ALICE: | But I didn't know you then. |
| TIGER-LILY: | Precisely! Didn't give us a second thought, did you. |
| ALICE: | But I was somewhere else! |
| VIOLET: | Exactly! Had something better to do, didn't you. |
| ALICE: | But I can't change the past! |
| TIGER-LILY: | Can't do much, can you. |
| ALICE: | It's not my fault! |
| VIOLET: | Never is, is it. |
| ALICE: | I just want to be your friend *now!* |
| TIGER-LILY: | Oh of course you do, now we've grown and have petals and look so pretty and smell so sweet, *everyone* wants to be our friend *now.* |
| ALICE: | But I'm *not* everyone! |
| TIGER-LILY: | Who *are* you then, if you're not everyone? |
| VIOLET: | Are you anyone? |
| ROSE: | Are you no one? |
| ALICE: | I'm *Alice!* I'm *Alice!* And I don't know where I am! |

*ALICE sinks down to the ground, weeping*

| | |
|---|---|
| TIGER-LILY: | What on earth is she doing? |
| VIOLET: | She's sort of fallen over. |
| TIGER-LILY: | No roots, you see, no stem. |
| ROSE: | Perhaps she's tired and she's taking a breather. |

| | |
|---|---|
| TIGER-LILY: | Take-take-take, that's all she ever does. |
| ROSE: | Oh look at her eyes, that's clever. |
| VIOLET: | What's she doing? |
| ROSE: | It's like drops of blood, but clear drops instead of red, there's one in each eye. Oh now there's two – three! |
| VIOLET: | You mean like dew in the early morning? |
| ROSE: | It's a little bit like dew in the early morning, but also quite like rain at dusk. |
| TIGER-LILY: | The Duchess! |
| VIOLET/ROSE: | The Duchess! |

*Enter the DUCHESS. The FLOWERS run away*

| | |
|---|---|
| DUCHESS: | Rain? Rain? *I've* seen rain, compared with which *that* would be like sunbeams. |
| ALICE: | Please, please Mrs Duchess, can you tell me where I am? |
| DUCHESS: | Mind your own business. If everybody minded their own business, the world would go round a good deal faster than it does. There, that's better. Off we go! |

*The DUCHESS starts running, as scenery starts moving past them*

| | |
|---|---|
| DUCHESS: | Run! Run! |
| ALICE: | I beg your pardon? |
| DUCHESS: | The world turns, did you not know that? |
| ALICE: | Of *course* I know it! |
| DUCHESS: | Then you'd better start running! |
| ALICE: | But we're not going anywhere. In *my* country you'd get somewhere else if you ran like this. |
| DUCHESS: | A slow sort of country! Here it takes all the running you can do just to keep in the same place. Run! Run! |

*ALICE joins in running*

ALICE:        This is nonsense!

DUCHESS:      Nonsense? *I've* heard nonsense compared
              with which *that* would be sensible as a
              dictionary. Faster, faster!

*The scenery is going away from them again*

ALICE:        But the world always turned before – I never
              had to do this!

DUCHESS:      Exactly! You didn't care! And the world
              won't stand for it! Run, it's turning faster!

*A DODO comes past in the moving scenery*

ALICE:        Look, a dodo!

DUCHESS:      Of course it's a dodo, who hasn't seen a
              dodo?

ALICE:        But there's no such things as dodos!

DUCHESS:      That's because he didn't run! He couldn't
              keep up!

ALICE:        Run faster, Mr Dodo! Run faster this time!

*The DODO runs off*

ALICE:        Oh *I* can't keep up, there'll be no such thing
              as me, oh I want to go home!

DUCHESS:      Never heard of it.

ALICE:        Home? It's where one lives!

DUCHESS:      *One* lives? It sounds lonely.

ALICE:        I mean where *people* live!

DUCHESS:      Oh so people have moved in? Sounds noisy.

ALICE:        I mean it's where *you* live!

DUCHESS:      How d'you know where I live, have you
              been listening at doors?

*TWEEDLEDEE and TWEEDLEDUM run past in the scenery*

ALICE:        Hey, you little boys, where are you going?

T'DUM:        We are not little boys, nohow!

| | |
|---|---|
| T'DEE: | Contrariwise! We are little men! We are two little men and we're having a race! |
| T'DUM: | Nohow! We are having a race and we're two little men! |
| ALICE: | But you're out of breath, why don't you rest a while? |
| T'DEE: | Because if I lose, he wins! |
| T'DUM: | Nohow! If I win, he loses! |
| ALICE: | Why does it all have to be about winning and losing? |

*They look at each other without a clue*

| | |
|---|---|
| T'DUM: | I've got a nice new rattle. |
| T'DEE: | Contrariwise, it's rubbish. |
| T'DUM: | It's the best there is! |
| T'DEE: | It's the worst there is! |

*Off they run, squabbling*

| | |
|---|---|
| ALICE: | Oh, when will we catch up with the world? |
| DUCHESS: | When I say so! |
| ALICE: | Why does the world have to wait for *you?* |
| DUCHESS: | Why? *Stop!* Because I'm a Duchess. |

*They stop running and the scenery stands still*

| | |
|---|---|
| ALICE: | Oh I'm thirsty now… |
| DUCHESS: | Drink your drink. |
| ALICE: | I already drank my drink, and it made me feel quite small. |
| DUCHESS: | You are quite small. |
| ALICE: | I mean it made me feel like I'd never get home. |
| DUCHESS: | *She probably never will, she's such a stupid creature.* Ah that's better. |
| ALICE: | I beg your pardon? |

DUCHESS:     Couldn't hear myself think. *Where on earth is her school uniform? That blue dress is ridiculous.*

ALICE:       Please, Mrs Duchess, I don't *want* to hear you think.

DUCHESS:     Oh, *very* convenient. *DRINK THE DRINK!*

ALICE:       Yes ma'am, I mean, your Grace, very well...

*ALICE drinks more from the bottle*

DUCHESS:     That's better, isn't it.

ALICE:       No.

DUCHESS:     I mean better for me. Would you listen to that... absolute silence.

ALICE:       I beg your pardon?

DUCHESS:     I'm trying to hear *you* think.

ALICE:       But I don't make any noise when I think!

DUCHESS:     That explains a lot.

ALICE:       No one can hear other people's thoughts! It's impossible. And I don't believe impossible things.

DUCHESS:     I daresay you haven't had much practice. When I was your age, I did it for half-an-hour each day. Sometimes I've believed as many as six impossible things before breakfast.

ALICE:       But with respect, you're a Duchess. And in any case I don't *want* you to hear what I'm thinking.

DUCHESS:     I'm not surprised, given the rubbish you speak. The Queen will know of this. *DRINK THE DRINK!*

*ALICE drinks again from the bottle*

DUCHESS:     That's better, isn't it.

| | |
|---|---|
| ALICE: | No – your Grace – I mean yes (I feel so very small now, it's like *everyone's* the Bully…) |
| DUCHESS: | Ah, good, now I can hear what you're thinking. |
| ALICE: | I *wasn't* thinking, I was talking. |
| DUCHESS: | You see that's your problem. I tend to do both things. Or sometimes neither. Go on thinking, I'm listening. |
| ALICE: | (It's really none of her business.) |
| DUCHESS: | *WHAT???* |
| ALICE: | I'm sorry, I was thinking, that wasn't meant to be heard out loud, it's just, I was wondering, which Queen do you mean? |
| DUCHESS: | Which Queen do I mean? |
| ALICE: | I mean, the Red one that's savage, or, or, the White one who doesn't believe in anything – |
| DUCHESS: | If those are your thoughts you can keep them to yourself. |
| ALICE: | I was really trying! |
| DUCHESS: | You're exceptionally trying. |
| ALICE: | But the drink makes me feel small, and makes me feel weak, and makes me want to cry and tell you how I feel, |
| DUCHESS: | Oh *very* convenient. |
| ALICE: | And, and, and then I was thinking how I *wish* I could see a friendly face, and then – then I saw one – it's over there! Look! |

*The CAT appears*

| | |
|---|---|
| ALICE: | Look, your Grace! |
| DUCHESS: | I *am* looking. |
| ALICE: | You're not looking at *that!* |
| DUCHESS: | Don't split hairs. |

| | |
|---|---|
| ALICE: | I mean you're looking the wrong way! |
| DUCHESS: | It's not the wrong way it's the right way. I'm quite happy with the way I look. |
| ALICE: | It's smiling! Ah… Please – can you tell me why your cat smiles like that? |
| DUCHESS: | No. I can't. |
| ALICE: | I've never seen a cat smile. In fact, I didn't know cats *could* smile. |
| DUCHESS: | They all can, and most of 'em do. |
| ALICE: | I don't know of any that do. |
| DUCHESS: | You don't know much and that's a fact. But then I'm listening to your thoughts and I hear absolutely nothing. Goodbye. |
| ALICE: | May I stay and play with your cat? |
| DUCHESS: | No. You can't. |
| ALICE: | Why ever not? |
| DUCHESS: | It's not my cat. |

*The DUCHESS goes*

| | |
|---|---|
| ALICE: | Pss-pss, pss-pss, here puss, pss-pss… |
| CAT: | What a peculiar sound you make. |
| ALICE: | You can talk! |
| CAT | *You* can talk. |
| ALICE: | Of course I can. May I ask you why are you smiling? |
| CAT: | I am not smiling. I am grinning. |
| ALICE: | Oh. So what's the difference between a smile and a grin? |
| CAT: | I don't have time for riddles. |
| ALICE: | It's not a riddle, I truly want to know! |
| CAT: | Very well. A smile is like a picnic, it's meant for sharing. A grin is like a packed lunch, you keep it to yourself. |

ALICE:     I – see. So. Why are you grinning?

CAT:       Because I know something interesting.
           The name of Cheshire derives from an early
           name for Chester, which was *Lege-ceaster-scir*,
           in the Anglo-Saxon Chronicle, meaning *the
           shire of the city of legions*.

ALICE:     Oh. Right… That *is* – interesting.

CAT:       Although the name first appears in the year
           980, it is thought that the county was created
           by Edward the Elder around the year 920.

ALICE:     Well I know what kind of cat *you* are, with all
           your information about Cheshire.

CAT:       Enlighten me, do.

ALICE:     You're an Information Cat!

CAT:       What else would you like to know?

ALICE:     All sorts of things! Everything!

CAT:       I mean about Cheshire.

ALICE:     Oh. I'm not sure. Is it not my turn now?

CAT:       You see, the Domesday Book records
           Cheshire as having two regions called
           Atiscross and Exestan, which later became
           the principal part of Flintshire.

ALICE:     That *is* interesting, isn't it.

CAT:       Not in the slightest, but I do know it.

ALICE:     And now I know it too, I'm sure it will come
           in useful.

CAT:       I doubt it, it never has before. I was on trial
           once, before the Red Queen, and I tried
           to explain to her that the eastern half of
           Cheshire is Upper Triassic Mercia Mudstone
           with large salt deposits, but to no avail.

ALICE:     Is she *very* savage, the Red Queen?

| | |
|---|---|
| CAT: | The distinctive local red sandstone has been used for many monuments. |
| ALICE: | That's not an answer! |
| CAT: | It's an answer to something. |
| ALICE: | I suppose. It's been nice talking to you, Cat, but I'm on my way home now, home to my house in England, can you tell me which way I ought to go from here? |
| CAT: | You must go north. |
| ALICE: | Thank you! |
| CAT: | And you must go south. |
| ALICE: | But those are – opposite ways. |
| CAT: | Well you did say England. |
| ALICE: | Yes, England, in the United Kingdom. |
| CAT: | There you go. |
| ALICE: | Well – can you tell me, Cat, my friend, if you would, what sort of people live around here? |
| CAT: | In that direction there lives a Hatter. And in that direction there lives a Hare. |
| ALICE: | Oh, and which one do you think would be more friendly? |
| CAT: | Neither, they're both mad. |
| ALICE: | But – I don't want to go among mad people. |
| CAT: | You can't help it, we're all mad here. They're mad, I'm mad, you're mad. |
| ALICE: | Why do you say I'm mad? |
| CAT: | You must be, or you wouldn't have come. |
| ALICE: | But I followed the White Rabbit! |
| CAT: | He's the maddest of all, he thinks time is still passing. No, we're all mad here. Except for the White Queen. |

| | |
|---|---|
| ALICE: | But she doesn't believe in anything! |
| CAT: | Yes well there's mad, and then there's very, very frightening. Goodbye. |
| ALICE: | But I thought we'd be best friends! |

*Despondent and lonely, ALICE sings a song about the Golden Afternoon she left behind. The CAT reappears*

| | |
|---|---|
| CAT: | Have some cake. |
| ALICE: | Pardon? |
| CAT: | You've had too much to drink. You're too small. Have some cake. But don't eat too much of that either. |
| ALICE: | How will I know when to stop? |
| CAT: | Stop once you've started, and by no means before. |
| ALICE: | That makes no sense, Cat. |
| CAT: | Have some cake. |
| ALICE: | Is it lunchtime? |
| CAT: | Lunchtime's over. Time for Tea. |

*The CAT disappears and ALICE is all alone*

*She opens up the packed lunch and starts unwrapping the cake. She bites into the cake*

| | |
|---|---|
| ALICE: | Oh yes! I like that. In fact I feel much better! Oh, I know one shouldn't talk with one's mouth full. But then again, it's not as if anyone's looking, it's not as if I'm at a tea party. |

*The Tea-Party rapidly assembles behind her. The HATTER, the HARE and the DORMOUSE run in and take their places at one end of the long table. ALICE sits down at the other end*

| | |
|---|---|
| ALL: | *NO ROOM! NO ROOM!* |
| ALICE: | There's plenty of room! |
| HARE: | Have some cordial. |

| | |
|---|---|
| ALICE: | I don't see any cordial. |
| HARE: | There isn't any. |
| ALICE: | Then it wasn't very civil of you to offer it. |
| HARE: | It wasn't very civil of you to sit down without being invited. |
| ALICE: | I didn't know it was *your* table, it's laid for a great many more than three. |
| HATTER: | *[With his mouth full.]* It wasn't very civil of her to talk with her mouth full. |
| ALICE: | It isn't very civil of you to talk like I'm not here! Also I didn't know I had company. |
| HARE: | Your hair wants cutting. |
| ALICE: | My hair is none of your business, Mr Hare. And you should learn not to make personal remarks, it's very rude. |
| HATTER: | Why is a raven like a writing-desk? |
| ALICE: | Pardon? |
| HATTER: | Why is a raven like a writing-desk? |
| ALICE: | I don't have time for riddles. |
| HATTER: | It's not a riddle, I truly want to know. |
| ALICE: | Well I don't have time to know, Mr Hatter, and I don't have time to *not* know! |
| HARE: | You mean *not to know.* |
| ALICE: | Do I, I don't know – |
| HATTER: | You had time to not know that. |
| HARE: | You mean time *not to know* that. |
| ALICE: | Does he? |
| HATTER: | What else do you have time for? |
| DORMOUSE: | *TEA!!!* |
| HATTER: | *ALL CHANGE!!!* |
| ALL: | *Will you won't you, will you won't you* |

*Will you join the dance?*
*Will you won't you, will you won't you.*
*Will you join the dance?*

*The HATTER, HARE and DORMOUSE get up, move some places along – forcing ALICE to do the same – and sit down again, the DORMOUSE going straight back to sleep. ALICE eats some more of the cake, which is giving her new confidence*

| | |
|---|---|
| HATTER: | I give up. |
| ALICE: | I beg your pardon? |
| HATTER: | I give up, why *is* a raven like a writing-desk? |
| ALICE: | I didn't set that riddle, *you* did, Mr Hatter, and I don't know, and I don't *care*, what's more! |
| HATTER: | That's not more, that's less. |
| HARE: | Less? It's nothing at all. |
| ALICE: | I think you might do something better with the time than waste it in asking riddles that have no answers. |
| HATTER: | If you knew Time as well as I do, you wouldn't talk about wasting *it*. It's a *him*. |
| ALICE: | I don't know what you mean! |
| HATTER: | Of course you don't. I daresay you never even spoke to Time. |
| ALICE: | Spoke to time? I know how to *keep* time, when I play the piano. |
| HATTER: | Ah, you see that's it, he won't be kept. He likes to be free. |
| ALICE: | Yes, you mean, as in – free time! |
| HATTER: | Exactly! WHAT DO WE WANT??? |
| HARE: | FREE! TIME! |
| HATTER: | WHEN DO WE WANT IT??? |
| HARE: | I dunno, whenever… |

HATTER: But then there's people like you, who want to *keep* Time, and some people *mark* Time, and some people *beat* Time, and one terrible person even –

HARE: Sshh! Don't tell her!

ALICE: Don't tell me what?

HARE: Don't tell her that.

HATTER: Don't tell her what?

HARE: Don't tell her *whooom...*

HATTER: *Whooom...*

DORMOUSE: *Whooom...*

ALICE: Oh I really want to know now, I'm curious!

HATTER: You said you didn't have time to know.

ALICE: Well, that was then, but this is now.

HATTER: No, *that* was then, and *this* is now.

HARE: Actually *that* was then and *this* is now.

ALICE: What did the terrible person do to Time?

HARE: Don't tell her! Don't say the word!

ALICE: You don't have to say the word, Mr Hatter, you can make it like a game, just tell me what the thing *begins* with, the thing that the terrible person did to Time...

HARE: Ah, very clever, very clever that.

ALICE: What does the thing begin with?

HATTER: *What does 'The Thing' begin with...*

DORMOUSE: *T!!!*

HATTER: *ALL CHANGE!!!*

ALL: *Will you won't you, will you won't you*
*Will you join the dance?*
*Will you won't you, will you won't you.*
*Will you join the dance?*

*They all move around again and ALICE eats more cake as she goes, angrily, greedily, she is losing self-control*

HATTER:    What week of the day is it?

ALICE:    I don't know!

HARE:    What year of the month is it?

ALICE:    I don't care!

HATTER:    Why is a raven like a writing-desk?

ALICE:    *IT'S NONE OF YOUR BUSINESS!*

*She shocks them, and herself too. She drinks from the bottle*

ALICE:    Oh… I'm most terribly sorry. I think I've
          eaten a little too much cake. I really wasn't
          myself just then. This will calm me down.
          There, that's better. I'm sorry. I wonder,
          pray, would you be so kind as to tell me
          what the terrible person did to Time?

*A pause, and then the HATTER starts weeping into his tea-cup*

HARE:    You've done it now.

ALICE:    What have I done?

HARE:    I just told you: It. Now.

ALICE.    But what's the matter with the Hatter?

HARE:    Oh that's rather good. *What's the matter with
          the Hatter…*

ALICE:    Don't you care, Mr Hare?

HARE:    Oh I *say*, you're on a roll!

ALICE:    What?

HARE:    You're sitting on my bread-roll, I've been
          looking for that everywhere.

ALICE:    Oh for heaven's sake, why's he crying?

HARE:    Well, as you're fond of saying, it's none of
          your business.

ALICE:  It *is* my business if I made him cry.
Mr Hatter, are you all right? I'm sorry,
I *would* like to hear the answer to your very
interesting riddle: why *is* a raven like a
writing-desk?

HARE:  That's an excellent impression.

ALICE:  Pardon?

HARE:  Oh yes, you have all his mannerisms.

ALICE:  It's not meant to be an impression!

HARE:  You got him just right, you got him down to
a –

DORMOUSE:  *TEE!!!*

HATTER:  *ALL CHANGE!!!*

ALL:  *Will you won't you, will you won't you*
*Will you join the dance?*
*Will you won't you, will you won't you.*
*Will you join the dance?*

*They all move round again, the HATTER's mood completely restored*

HATTER:  Well I'll tell you. It was at the Great Concert
given by the Red Queen, and I had to sing
*Twinkle Twinkle Little Bat, How I wonder what*
*you're at,* you know the song, perhaps?

ALICE:  I know a *version* of it...

HATTER:  Well I'd scarcely finished the eleventh verse
when the Queen jumped up and bawled out
*He's killing Time! Off with his head!*

ALICE:  How dreadfully savage!

HATTER:  Isn't it? And Time believed her, and ever
since that day he won't do a thing I ask of
him. So it's always four o'clock. And the
table's always set for tea. And we never have
time to wash the plates.

ALICE:  Is that why you keep moving round the table?

| | |
|---|---|
| HATTER: | No. |
| ALICE: | Why *do* you keep moving round the table? |
| HARE: | We don't. |
| ALICE: | But you just did. |
| HARE: | No we didn't. |
| HATTER: | Do we *look* like we're moving round the table? |
| ALICE: | Well no, not now, but I saw you, just then! |
| HARE: | Living in the past, she is. |
| HATTER: | Where *does* she get her information? |
| ALICE: | With my own eyes and ears! |
| HARE: | Her *own* eyes, you notice, her *own* ears. |
| HATTER: | That explains it, totally self-centred. |
| HARE: | Living in a bubble. |
| HATTER: | I think it's sad. |
| ALICE: | Well I'm going to finish my cake, and, and *never* come here again, because it's the stupidest tea-party I ever was at in all my life! |
| HATTER: | Me too! |
| HARE: | Me four! |
| HATTER: | Hear hear! |
| HARE: | There there! |
| HATTER: | And don't forget what comes after T! |
| ALICE: | I don't know – what *does* come after tea? |
| DORMOUSE: | *U!!!* |
| HATTER: | *ALL CHANGE!!!* |

*The Tea Party is rapidly disassembled and ALICE is all alone again*

| | |
|---|---|
| ALICE: | Well I do know one thing. If I missed lunch, and that was tea, and now it's after tea, then the end of the day can't be far away. And |

then it's home time – oh, *home*-time… It's
high time it was home-time. But how do I get
to home from here? My best friend is the Cat
and even he couldn't say. Oh – and what did
Lory tell me about the end of the school day?
The Great Big Bully… looking for new girls,
waiting at the end of classes! Whatever will I
do? Cake, cake. Maybe I won't feel quite so
afraid.

*She has some more cake. Three RED PAWNS come, PAWN 2, PAWN 5
and PAWN 7, and start setting up the space for a Trial. But they only
move one step forward at a time, being pawns*

ALICE:     There! You see, three giant red pawns just
           appeared and I'm not afraid in the slightest.

PAWN 2:    Three giant red pawns, she goes.

PAWN 5:    Not upset in the slightest, she goes.

PAWN 7:    There's going to be a Trial, she goes.

ALICE:     I didn't say 'There's going to be a Trial.'

PAWN 5:    I think that was you, Seven.

PAWN 7:    It was? I don't even know any more.

ALICE:     *Is* there going to be a Trial?

PAWN 7:    Is there going to be a Trial, he goes.

ALICE:     No, *I* said that. You ought to pay more
           attention, Mr Pawn.

PAWN 5:    I think she's talking to you, Three.

PAWN 2:    I *am* payin' attention, and I ain't Three
           I'm Two.

PAWN 7:    It must be you then, Six.

PAWN 5:    I ain't Six, I'm Five!

PAWN 7:    That's exactly what I mean! She doesn't
           know who we are, so she just says 'Mr Pawn',
           and *you* don't know who *he* is because you
           just called him Eight, and *I* don't know who
           *you* are because I just called you Five!

| | |
|---|---|
| PAWN 5: | No I *am* Five, mate, but you just called me Six. |
| PAWN 7: | I'm sorry, Six. |
| PAWN 5: | *Five!!!* |
| PAWN 7: | No one can tell us apart! Because we're Pawns – and we used to be Hearts! I used to be the Seven! And now I'm just a number! |
| ALICE: | You mean you used to be a number and now you're nothing. |
| PAWN 7: | Oh rub it in, why don't you. |
| PAWN 5: | *[To ALICE.]* What are you, some kind of Rook? |
| PAWN 7: | Yes and what sort of colour do you call that? |
| ALICE: | Blue, I call it blue. |
| PAWN 5: | What's *blue* when it's at home? |
| ALICE: | Well – it's this! |
| PAWN 5: | Why d'you call it *blue* then, why don't you just say *this*? |
| ALICE: | Um… well *[pointing at the sky]* it's also that! |
| PAWN 5: | Oh so it's *that* as well as *this*, is it? Very slippery notion… |
| PAWN 2: | Seven's got a point though. I was the Two… The *Deuce*, they used to call me, ah, made me feel good that did, the *Deuce,* and you was the Five, we was all different like. And you was like, *higher*, but in some games that was a bad thing, and sometimes the Deuce of Hearts was just what the Queen needed, and *I've got the Deuce*, she'd say, then she'd play me and win the hand, oh them golden nights… |
| ALICE: | That's very sweet, but I don't understand, are you talking about the Red Queen? Are you saying she used to be the Queen of Hearts? |

PAWN 5:    In the old days she did. And we used to play
           games with the Diamonds and Spades and
           them other fellers with the weird bobbly
           heads.

PAWN 7:    Ah yes, but she took against them all, one
           by one. She found the Diamonds too flashy,
           and the Spades kept digging dirt on her,
           and the Clubs were, you know, just full of
           themselves.

PAWN 2:    So she got rid of 'em all!

PAWN 5:    Changed the game, she did.

PAWN 7:    Now there's us, the Reds, and there's them,
           the Others, the Whites, and it's all much
           simpler.

PAWN 5:    Yeah these days we know who's good and
           who's bad.

PAWN 7:    Who's in and who's out.

PAWN 2:    Who's right an' who's wrong.

PAWN 7:    It's really very simple. If you look like me
           you're right and if you look like someone
           else you're wrong. That's an intellectual
           position, you know.

PAWN 5:    And there's a poem to help you remember!

ALICE:     A poem? What do you mean?

PAWN 7:    It's simple. *R is for Red and R is for Right.*

PAWN 5:    *R is for Red and R is for Right.* That's our
           anthem, that is.

PAWN 2:    Wait, R is for *Wrong*, innit?

PAWN 5:    Not this again.

PAWN 2:    It's W for Write and W for… wong. No wait.

PAWN 7:    Oh good grief.

PAWN 5:    It's R for Red and R for White. Hang on
           that's wong, I mean wrong –

| | |
|---|---|
| PAWN 7: | *Will you shut up, Two!!!* |
| PAWN 2: | *I'm* Two! |
| PAWN 5: | I'm Five and no I won't! |
| ALICE: | *Will you all be quiet!* |
| PAWN 2: | Shall I take her, Five? |
| PAWN 5: | Yeah go on, she's asking for it. |

*But ALICE knows chess and moves out of range, eats some more cake*

| | |
|---|---|
| PAWN 2: | That's annoying. |
| ALICE: | Come on then, take me, little Pawn. Out of your reach, aren't I? |
| PAWN 2: | I was the *Deuce of Hearts,* I was. |
| ALICE: | Look I'm sorry for your troubles, but I have troubles too. You see I'm trying to get home. |
| PAWN 7: | What, to become a Queen? Respect. |
| PAWN 2: | Does that mean she's one of us? |
| PAWN 5: | No way. |
| PAWN 2: | Then she's one of them! Let's take her! |

*ALICE moves out of their reach again*

| | |
|---|---|
| ALICE: | I don't want to become a Queen, I want to go home, to Edie and mummy and now you say there's going to be a Trial. Who exactly is on trial? |
| PAWN 2: | Who is it, Five, who's gettin' executed? |
| ALICE: | *Executed?* Shouldn't the evidence come first? |
| PAWN 5: | The evidence first! She said the evidence comes first! Ha! |
| PAWN 7: | Sentence first, verdict next, evidence last! |
| PAWN 2: | Lads, someone's coming, it's her, it's her! |

*The PAWNS throw themselves on the ground in fear. But the not-at-all-fearsome RED KING waddles in instead. They look up, totally relax*

RED KING: Oh yes, on your feet, that's right, do things. All Hail his Majesty the Red King! *All Hail! Bam-pa-daaa!*

ALICE: Shouldn't someone else be doing that for you?

RED KING: Um, traditionally that's true, but trumpets are expensive, and you know, there've been modernizations. As long as it gets said, eh… Hang on, who are you? On your knees!

ALICE: I don't think so.

RED KING: No! Indeed! Stand there then. I command you to stand there!

ALICE: Very well, I shall. May I ask you who's on Trial?

RED KING: No. Silence! *[Pause.]* End of silence! *Bam-pa-daaa!*

ALICE: Perhaps if you *commanded* me to ask you who's on Trial?

RED KING: Yes! Good, I *command* you to ask me who's on Trial!

ALICE: Who's on Trial.

RED KING: I've no idea. But a good question. I do know the Accusations, mind, I have them written down, where are they, I think we're still looking for someone to fit them…

ALICE: To fit the Accusations?

RED KING: Yes, look, I did them in lots of different colours and I think it looks rather good. (Well done, Your Majesty. Thank you, you're welcome.) *Bam-pa-daaa!*

ALICE: Stop doing that. *Various Accusations…*

RED KING: Yes, if you can think of anyone who fits the bill I'd rather appreciate it if you'd let me know.

| ALICE: | Very well. Number One: *Failure to Wear Uniform.* |
| RED KING: | That's ten years right there. |
| ALICE: | Two: *Failure to Complete Homework.* |
| RED KING: | Sixteen years in solitary. |
| ALICE: | Three: *Thinking in Silence.* |
| RED KING: | That's Execution. |
| ALICE: | Four: *Having One's Cake and Eating It.* |
| RED KING: | That's Execution *plus* sixteen years. |
| ALICE: | That would be a very strange sixteen years… |
| RED KING: | I don't see why. Do you like the colours I've chosen? |
| ALICE: | Everything's red. |
| RED KING: | You've read everything? Good. Now, do you know anyone who fits the bill? |
| ALICE: | I do. |
| RED KING: | And who might that be? |
| ALICE: | I said *I* do. *I* fit the bill. |
| RED KING: | *She fits the Bill!* |
| PAWNS: | *SHE FITS THE BILL!!!* |
| ALL: | *SENTENCE FIRST! VERDICT NEXT! EVIDENCE LAST! OFF WITH HER HEAD!!!* |

*The Trial is set up, and four WITNESSES run in – the CATERPILLAR, TIGER-LILY, the DUCHESS and the HATTER. ALICE is now greedily cramming cake into her mouth*

| ALICE: | Stuff and nonsense! The idea of having the sentence first! The evidence is first! |
| RED KING: | Call the First Witness! |
| W RABBIT: | She doesn't even know the Queen. |
| ALICE: | I plead guilty. |
| RED KING: | Next Witness! |

| | |
|---|---|
| TIGER-LILY: | She *said* she had a friend called Leesha in the meadow… |
| ALICE: | I plead guilty! |
| RED KING: | Next Witness! |
| DUCHESS: | She said she wants to go home! |
| ALICE: | Guilty! |
| RED KING: | Next Witness! |
| HATTER: | She said we moved round the table! She's living in the past! |
| ALICE: | *GUILTY!* Yes I'm guilty! Off with my head! I *was* with Mary by the river, and I did meet a friend called Leesha in the meadow, and I do want to go home right now and if that's living in the past then that's where I want to be! |
| ALL: | She's mad! She's mad! Fetch the Queen! The Queen! |
| ALICE: | Fetch whom you like! I didn't want to come here! I didn't want to come to this stupid ridiculous school of yours, I didn't want to come to any boring-school at all, I wanted to lay down in the meadow with Edie and mummy and Lory forever, and play, and dress up, and hide and seek and make-believe, and hear stories by the river in the golden sunshine, and never see the clouds come, or the sunset come or the night fall, and I didn't want to take the train, or wear the uniform, or do my homework, and I only found one friend all day and I can't find him now, and everyone else is horrid and cruel and talks in riddles, and it's not fair, it's not fair, it's not fair and *I won't have it!* |

*All surround her angrily as she bolts the last of the cake, puts the cake-tin on her head and wraps herself in the great red carpet*

| | |
|---|---|
| RED KING: | I say, somebody do something! |
| ALICE: | *SILENCE IN THE COURT!* |
| W RABBIT: | You're late! You're late! |
| ALICE: | *SPEAK WHEN YOU'RE SPOKEN TO!* |
| DUCHESS: | A nasty, vicious temper. |
| ALICE: | *HOLD YOUR TONGUE!* |
| HATTER: | I'm a poor man, your Majesty – |
| ALICE: | *OFF WITH HIS HEAD!!! OFF WITH HER HEAD!!! OFF WITH YOUR HEAD!!! OFF WITH ALL YOUR HEADS!!!* |

*The WONDERLAND CREATURES flee in terror, as ALICE storms off*

*Elsewhere ALICIA, in a white night-dress, wakes from her coma and sits up in bed*

| | |
|---|---|
| ALICIA: | Alice? |

*Blackout*

# ACT TWO

## 3 – ALICIA IN WONDERLAND

*ALICIA asleep in bed, in a white night-dress. Her MOTHER and*
*a DOCTOR at her bedside*

MOTHER: *Alice* – that was the first word I understood
– *Alice, wait for me!* she cried – then she just –
lay down and was gone again.

DOCTOR: Hmm, her own name… Interesting…

MOTHER: Yes, but she's been worried about her name,
doctor. Her real name is *Alicia,* and she
was supposed to be starting her new school
today, where she *would* be Alicia, but she
does like to be *Alice,* it was troubling her so.
I was going to tell her she could choose a
new name, it was to be a surprise.

DOCTOR: Choose a *new* name? That sounds rather –
progressive.

MOTHER: Thank you.

DOCTOR: That's not what I meant.

MOTHER: I know.

DOCTOR: Starting a new school today… I see.
Interesting timing, don't you think?

MOTHER: Her temperature is 103°, doctor. You said so
yourself.

DOCTOR: True, true… What about this clasping of the
hands together?

MOTHER: I don't know. She's been like that for hours.

DOCTOR: I've not encountered this in my training.

MOTHER: You'll have to use your mind then.

DOCTOR: I've not encountered this in my training.

MOTHER: You'll have to use your mind then.

*The MOTHER and DOCTOR are frozen in time. ALICIA gets out of bed*

ALICIA: Hello, mother. Dr Proctor. I must have a fever. That's why everything looks like a tableau. I'm going to find Alice now, she needs me, silly girl. I last saw her in the picnic meadow.

*ALICIA walks on to the Picnic Meadow, now in an otherly light*

ALICIA: This looks like the place, but it *feels* nothing like it. I know why that is. I'm seeing it on a school day, I'm not supposed to be here at all. This must be the world of grown-ups. It's very still and nobody's playing. Now where was the gap she went through…

*ALICIA tries to find the place where she lost Alice. Suddenly the WHITE RABBIT – now actually a RED RABBIT – runs by*

ALICIA: Stop! I say stop!

W RABBIT: No I mustn't, I'll be late! The Queen will be savage if I keep her waiting!

ALICIA: Now this time you really *are* looking at your watch, but that's because I have a fever, I'm seeing all sorts of things.

W RABBIT: Please – I have to go – oh my fur and whiskers, she'll have my head off!

ALICIA: Look at you, you're all red, and there's no such thing as a red rabbit. Explain yourself.

*Though terrified, the WHITE RABBIT can't resist whispering a secret*

W RABBIT: *We… have to be red.*

ALICIA: Why do you have to be red?

W RABBIT: *Because… everything is red.*

ALICIA: What do you mean everything is red?

W RABBIT: Everything is… *read to us.* And if it's read to us we have to believe it!

ALICIA:     That sounds like a very dismal country.
            I'm glad it doesn't exist.

W RABBIT:   But it does! It's happening here!

ALICIA:     Silly bunny, I have a fever of 103° Fahrenheit,
            according to Dr Proctor, I'm very ill, which
            means I'm having ill-ucinations. So don't
            worry, you're not actually there at all.

*The WHITE RABBIT has a terrible realization*

W RABBIT:   *It's – you! – it's her! You're you! YOU'RE
            HER!!! THE WHITE QUEEN!!!*

*The WHITE RABBIT flees*

ALICIA:     The White Queen? I should *like* to be a
            Queen, but I'm hardly dressed for it. If *I*
            wrote a story, bunnies would make a lot
            more sense. Alice? Alice it's Alicia, I've
            come to find you, I – I say, what on earth
            is that?

*The CAT appears*

ALICIA:     Is that a cat? Oh. Now it's gone again. What
            a very strange fever I'm suffering. And
            what's all that terrible commotion?

*We hear a fight starting, and then a LION (English) and a UNICORN
(Scottish) enter, duelling with swords*

ALICIA:     It's a Lion and a Unicorn! And they're
            fighting. How funny!

*They stop fighting*

LION:       Hold your horses, what the devil is funny
            about it?

ALICIA:     Well, it's just like the nursery rhyme, isn't it?

LION:       Not with you, sorry.

ALICIA:     *The Lion and the Unicorn were fighting for the
            crown, the Lion beat the Unicorn all around the
            town,*

| UNICORN: | Come *again*, lassie? |
|---|---|
| ALICIA: | *Some gave them white bread, some gave them brown, some gave them plum-cake and drummed them out of town.* D'you not know it? |
| LION: | Look, little girl, we're in the heat of battle here and you come swanning by, telling us it's funny! |
| UNICORN: | Aye, then trying to tell us the result, d'ye have a flutter on the outcome, by any chance? |
| LION: | Really, and then telling us what snacks we'll be having afterwards, it's *too* much! |
| UNICORN: | Gonna drum us out of here, are you? |
| LION: | Though there *was* a mention of plum-cake... |
| UNICORN: | What's your problem, lassie? |
| ALICIA: | My problem? I'm running a temperature of 104° Fahrenheit so I'm having ill-ucinations, and nursery rhymes are coming to life! |
| LION: | Have you *any* idea what she's talking about? |
| UNICORN: | Not a clue, pal. On we go. |
| LION: | Out of the way please, little girl. |

*They retake their martial stances*

| LION: | For the Crown! |
|---|---|
| UNICORN: | Aye, for the Crown! |
| ALICIA: | You're just a children's song about a coat of arms. The Lion of England and the Unicorn of Scotland. |
| LION: | Look, what the blazes does a little girl like *you* know about heraldry? |
| ALICIA: | Ah, well in terms of heraldry you're *royal supporters*, aren't you? |
| LION: | What the deuce does *that* mean? |

UNICORN:       You've lost me, lassie.

ALICIA:        You hold up the shield, don't you? *Supporters,*
               *dexter* (to the right) *a lion rampant, gardant*
               *Or* (meaning gold) *crowned as the Crest,* yes?
               That's you. *Sinister* (to the left) *a unicorn*
               *Argent* (meaning silver) *armed, crined and*
               *unguled Proper, gorged with a Coronet.* That's
               you.

*Pause*

LION:          I think we might take tea now.

UNICORN:       Aye, maybe something a wee bit stronger...

ALICIA:        It's amazing what things one knows when
               one's having ill-ucinations.

*The LION and the UNICORN wander off, sadly*

ALICIA:        I'm sorry, I didn't mean to spoil your fun!
               Just because you're not real, doesn't mean
               you can't enjoy yourselves! ...Oh well,
               never mind. Who ever knew that even with
               ill-ucinations one has to have good manners?
               I'll try to remember.

*The LIVE FLOWERS come*

ALICIA:        Oh look, now I *know* I'm lying in bed, safely
               at home, somebody's brought me flowers.
               Maybe Mary, or Lory and Edie...

TIGER-LILY:    We can *talk*, you know, when there's anyone
               worth –

ALICIA:        Of *course* you can talk, anyone can talk in ill-
               ucinations.

VIOLET:        *Anyone?* We're not just *anyone!*

ALICIA:        Oh a violet, how sweet. Your odour is used
               in the perfume industry.

VIOLET:        *WHAT* did you say?

| | |
|---|---|
| ALICIA: | It's known as a 'flirty' scent, as its fragrance comes and goes. |
| VIOLET: | *WHAT???* |
| ALICIA: | And you're extensively used in bedding. |
| VIOLET: | *BEDDING???* |

*VIOLET storms off, outraged*

| | |
|---|---|
| ALICIA: | But you're a Rose, ah, how nice. |
| ROSE: | I – yes, I am – |
| ALICIA: | I do like a rose. |
| ROSE: | Oh, yes, thank you – |
| ALICIA: | There are lots of you in my garden. |
| ROSE: | Oh, are there – |
| ALICIA: | You being so extremely common. |
| ROSE: | Common! |

*ROSE flees in floods of tears*

| | |
|---|---|
| ALICIA: | Excuse me, but, have you seen a girl in a blue dress who looks a bit like me? |
| TIGER-LILY: | You? And who do you think *you* are? |
| ALICIA: | I'm Alicia Liddell, and you're a Tiger Lily. Also known as the Roadside Lily or Ditch Lily – |
| TIGER-LILY: | The *ditch?* |
| ALICIA: | Or Outhouse Lily, as those are places you tend to be found. |
| TIGER-LILY: | That wasn't me! I wasn't there! |

*TIGER-LILY hurries off, embarrassed*

| | |
|---|---|
| ALICIA: | What's wrong with that? It's the truth after all. I am *trying* to be polite, you know. |

*The HATTER, HARE and DORMOUSE run in with a small table and four chairs. They continually rise, move round a place, sit, and do this again*

| | |
|---|---|
| ALICIA: | More imaginary friends! Good afternoon, may I sit down? |
| ALL: | *NO ROOM! NO ROOM!* |
| ALICIA: | There *is* room, there's lots of room! |
| HATTER: | It's for her! |
| ALICIA: | For whom? |
| HARE: | *Whooom…* |
| DORMOUSE: | *Whooom…* |
| HATTER: | For the Red Queen of course! She's very angry with us, I gave evidence at the Trial. We're not allowed to stop moving, and we have to keep a spare place for her at all times or it's off with our heads! |
| ALICIA: | Oh I see, well that's very interesting. But I wish you'd stop moving just for a moment, I've a question to ask. |
| HARE: | *No room!* |
| DORMOUSE: | *Whooom!* |
| HATTER: | We can only stop moving if you ask us a riddle. |
| ALICIA: | Very well, it's a riddle. |

*They stop abruptly*

| | |
|---|---|
| ALICIA: | Have you seen a girl looking a little bit like me, but sillier and wearing a blue dress? |
| ALL: | *I don't know, have we seen a girl looking a little bit like you, but sillier and wearing a blue dress!* |
| ALICIA: | Oh for heaven's sake… |
| HARE: | I can't *wait* for the answer to this one! |
| HATTER: | Psst, I've got one after that, it's about a writing-desk. |
| ALICIA: | Look it's not really a riddle, it's a question! |
| HATTER: | We don't answer questions. |

| | |
|---|---|
| HARE: | We don't question answers. |
| DORMOUSE: | *ALL CHANGE!* |
| ALICIA: | *STOP RIGHT THERE!* |

*Pause*

| | |
|---|---|
| HATTER: | You know what, she *does* look a little bit like Her… |
| HARE: | Sounds like Her, too… |
| HATTER: | Yes, if she were sillier and wearing a blue dress… |
| ALICIA: | Her? You're referring to whom? |
| DORMOUSE: | *Whooom…* |
| ALICIA: | Shut up. Where did you meet *Her?* |
| HATTER: | Well, that's an easy one. *[A whisper.]* We met *Her* the last time She came round for… |
| HARE | *[A whisper.]* The last time She came round for… |
| DORMOUSE | *[A whisper.] Tea…* |
| ALL: | *ALL CHANGE!* |

*They try to move round again, but ALICIA sits down in the spare place*

| | |
|---|---|
| ALICIA: | Stay right where you are. I know why you're all here. I have a temperature of 105° Fahrenheit, I am suffering ill-ucinations. You, sir *[the Hatter]* work in the millinery trade, and it's a well-known fact that in the treatment of felt you use mercury, excessive exposure to which can lead to a type of dementia. Hence the proverbial 'mad as a hatter'. You, sir *[the Hare]* are a Hare, or *lepus europaeus,* a species well-known for its energetic behaviour in the early spring, hence the proverbial 'mad as a March hare', and you, sir *[the Dormouse]* are a Dormouse, which has etymological associations with |

the French *dormir*, to sleep, and this, I believe, explains your participation and your behaviour in this particular ill-ucination.

*Pause*

HATTER:     Why is a raven like a writing-desk?

ALICIA:     I have news for you, Mr Hatter. A raven is nothing *like* a writing-desk.

*The HATTER, HARE and DORMOUSE are shocked by this heresy*

ALICIA:     *[A triumphant whisper.] All – change.*

*Distraught, they flee in different directions*

ALICIA:     Ha! that put them in their place. Why are people so afraid of the truth? … Alice? Alice can you hear me? It's so quiet here. At least they were some company, those silly phrases that came to life. Where's that Cat, that's the best ill-ucination of all.

*The CAT's face comes back, this time it is smiling*

ALICIA:     There it is!! I wonder what it's smiling about…

CAT:        Why don't you ask It.

ALICIA:     Oh it can talk! I mean – you can. Of course you can, there are no rules here, are there? Not at 106° Fahrenheit! Why are you smiling, Cat?

CAT:        Why am I smiling. Why are *you* smiling.

ALICIA:     Well, because *you're* smiling! In any case I asked you first.

CAT:        You did. I'm smiling because of the Anderton Boat Lift.

ALICIA:     The Anderson – I'm sorry, what?

CAT:        The Anderton Boat Lift in Anderton, Cheshire. It provides a vertical link between

two navigable waterways, the River Weaver
and the Trent and Mersey Canal.

ALICIA: I see. That's…interesting.

CAT: And in time it will allow Cheshire cheese
and rock-salt to become major county
exports.

ALICIA: Yes. I suppose it will.

CAT: This means nothing to you.

ALICIA: No. I suppose not.

CAT: You think it's a little thing, do you?

ALICIA: Well. Yes, to be honest. It's a little thing to
me. Sorry.

CAT: Only – you're still smiling.

ALICIA: Only because you are.

CAT: Then it *does* mean something to you.
It made me smile, which made you smile.
So, if it weren't for the Anderton Boat Lift
you wouldn't be smiling.

ALICIA: Look, there's nothing strange about smiling
at people who are smiling at you!

CAT: There is if you don't believe they exist.

ALICIA: Well I don't, really, but I like you anyway,
Cat!

CAT: Do you? Imagine what you could do for
people who *do* exist.

*The CAT vanishes*

ALICIA: I – I – don't go, Cat – let me explain! I'm
– not sure I *can* explain. I don't seem to –
know what I knew before… But if that Cat's
face just appeared in my mind, it must have
done so for a reason. Mother says I can learn
from everything. What did I just learn there?

*She looks around, shivers*

ALICIA:   Oh they come and go so fast, my ill-
          ucinations… And every time they go they
          leave a deeper silence, and the sky seems
          that much darker. Cat? Cat? That *was*
          interesting about the Anderson Boat Trip,
          it was, and the cheese, I *like* cheese, you
          know, you can tell me more about cheese
          if you like… I do believe you exist, you see!
          (I mean, in terms of being an image
          generated by my mind at 107° Fahrenheit)
          oh Alicia stop explaining things!

*ALICIA is increasingly nervous, and it's getting darker*

ALICIA:   Alice? Alice are you here somewhere? Alice?
          It's Alicia, or, well, *Leesha*, if you like, we
          can work on that later, together, and I'm
          sorry I didn't believe you about that Rabbit,
          I do believe in it now (I mean, in terms of
          it being a delusion symptomatic of my) oh
          stop it Alicia! Alice! Alice! I've come to –
          rescue you, will you – will you come and be
          rescued? Please?

*The band start to play the intro to her Golden Afternoon song*

ALICIA:   Would you stop that please. I'm not just
          going to break into song. That's not a thing
          that happens.

VOICES:   *[Off.] The sun was shining on the sea,*
          *Shining with all his might:*
          *He did his very best to make*
          *The billows smooth and bright –*
          *And this was odd, because it was*
          *The middle of the night.*

*ALICIA edges to where she thinks the VOICES are coming from*

ALICIA:   That's curious. But it made no sense at all,
          and it's not the middle of the night, it's the
          end of the – the end of the – the time after
          lunch that ends with dinner. That sort of

warm yellow time that goes blue in the end. Funny, I can't remember its name.

*While she ponders, TWEEDLEDEE and TWEEDLEDUM appear from the opposite direction and stand directly behind her, stock-still. When she finally sees them, she screams in fright*

| | |
|---|---|
| T'DUM: | If you think we're waxworks, you ought to pay, you know. Waxworks weren't made to be looked at for nothing. Nohow! |
| T'DEE: | Contrariwise. If you think we're alive, you ought to speak. |
| ALICIA: | I – I'm – I'm sure I'm very sorry. |

*She looks at the names on their collars*

| | |
|---|---|
| ALICIA: | Tweedledum... Tweedledee. Yes. (Alicia, remember, this is real to *them*) How does it go? *Tweedledum and Tweedledee agreed to have a battle; for Tweedledum said Tweedledee had spoiled his nice new rattle...* |
| T'DUM: | I did, and he did! True on both counts! |
| T'DEE: | Contrariwise! |
| T'DUM: | Nohow! |
| T'DEE: | If it was so, it might be, and if it were so, it would be, but as it isn't, it ain't. That's logic. |
| ALICIA: | Yes, very good, it's true, or it's not, now I wonder if you can tell me where I might find – |
| T'DUM: | She's begun wrong! The first thing in a visit is to say *How d'ye do* and shake hands! |

*She puts her hands out. Each grabs one hand, and they dance her round in a circle. They let go and she goes spinning, recovers*

| | |
|---|---|
| ALICIA: | Well I daresay this must be 108°, when your ill-ucinations start dancing with you... |

*TWEEDLEDUM shakes the broken rattle at TWEEDLEDEE*

| | |
|---|---|
| T'DUM: | Do you see that? |
| T'DEE: | It's only an old rattle. |

| | |
|---|---|
| T'DUM: | But it *isn't* old! It's *new*, it's a nice *new* rattle! Of course you agree to have a battle? |
| T'DEE: | I suppose so, and she'll decide the winner! |
| ALICIA: | *[To herself.]* And evidently at 109° one's ill-ucinations start taking one for granted. Now how does the *second* verse go… |
| T'DUM: | I'm very brave generally, only today I have a headache. |
| T'DEE: | I've got a toothache, I'm *far* worse off. All this for a rattle! |
| T'DUM: | I shouldn't have minded, if it hadn't been a new one. |
| ALICIA: | *[To herself.]* I remember: *Just then flew down a monstrous – something, as black as a something something…* A monstrous what? Does something eat them? |
| T'DEE: | Let's fight till five, and then have dinner. |
| T'DUM: | Nohow! Let's have dinner, and then fight till six. |
| T'DEE: | Contrariwise! Let's fight six and have dinner with five. |
| T'DUM: | Nohow! Five lets six and have fights for dinner. |
| ALICIA: | Stop, stop, you're just quarreling for the sake of it, but you don't have time! Something is coming to get you! You need to run away! |
| T'DUM: | Nohow. We've nowhere to go. |
| T'DEE: | Contrariwise. We've nowhere to stay. |
| T'DUM: | Nohow. We've nowhere to run. |
| T'DEE: | Contrariwise. We've nowhere to hide. |
| ALICIA: | But don't you see, you're both saying the same thing! Why can you never agree with each other? |

| | |
|---|---|
| T'DUM: | Nohow! We agree! |
| T'DEE: | Contrariwise. We don't! |
| T'DUM: | Nohow! We disagree! |
| T'DEE: | Contrariwise! We do! |
| ALICIA: | You just swap the same thing back and forth like a game, why can't you forget your little quarrels and be friends? |

*TWEEDLEDUM and TWEEDLEDEE look at each other*

| | |
|---|---|
| T'DUM: | You tell her. |
| T'DEE: | No you tell her. |
| T'DUM: | You first. |
| T'DEE: | No you first. |
| ALICE: | Please! |

*They gesture for ALICIA to come closer and she does. They whisper*

| | |
|---|---|
| T'DUM:/T'DEE: | *Because it would be so quiet.* |
| T'DEE: | No it wouldn't. |
| T'DUM: | Yes it would. |
| T'DEE: | Contrariwise! |
| T'DUM: | Nohow! |

*A shadow falls – TWEEDLEDUM and TWEEDLEDEE run away.*

*ALICIA crouches down as nothing comes and the danger passes*

| | |
|---|---|
| ALICIA: | At 110° one starts tumbling into other people's nursery-rhymes. Well, Cat, Cat? Did you see me? They weren't real, but I did try to help them! I even pretended to be afraid of the – something – when I know it was only in my mind! Cat, did I not do well? Who am I talking to? What's a – *cat?* I can't – remember how I got here. |
| VOICES: | *[Off] The sun was shining on the sea,*<br>*Shining with all his might...*<br>*He did his very best to make* |

73

*The billows smooth and bright...*
*And this was odd, because it was*
*The middle of the night...*

## 4 – JABBERWOCKY

*ALICIA, unnerved, cannot work out where the VOICES are coming from now. When they cease she hears the confused voice of ALICE from off*

ALICE:          *[Off.]* I beg your pardon... Nothing. Nothing whatever. It doesn't matter a bit...

*ALICE comes, still wrapped in the red carpet and crowned with the cake-tin, making no sense, talking to imaginary playing-cards*

ALICE:          I'm not a mile high.

ALICIA:         That's – that's – that's her... *Alice...*

ALICE:          I shan't go, at any rate.

ALICIA:         Alice, it's me, Leesha, I mean *Alicia...*

ALICE:          That's not a regular rule, you invented it just now.

ALICIA:         Alice, I've come to take you home.

ALICE:          It doesn't prove anything of the sort.

ALICIA:         Who are you talking to?

ALICE:          Whooom! That's not said right.

ALICIA:         Hush, that's true, that's very good, but there's no one there, dear, you're seeing things, it's all right, it's 111° Fahrenheit, I was seeing things too –

ALICE:          You don't even know what they're about!

ALICIA:         Ssh, ssh...

ALICE:          Cards, quick! It's the White Queen! She doesn't believe we're real!

ALICIA:         Alice I'm *not* the White Queen, I'm a girl in a night-dress.

ALICE:          Silence! Do you not know who I am?

ALICIA:    Alice…

ALICE:    I used to be the Red Queen – now I'm the
          Queen of Hearts because everybody loves
          me! Five? Seven? Oh my poor old *Deuce…* if
          any one of them can explain it I'll give him
          sixpence.

ALICIA:    Alice, it's nothing, nothing but a pack of
          cards, and it's getting rather dark now…

ALICE:    I don't believe there's an atom of meaning in it!

*ALICE breaks down and cries*

ALICE:    Off with their heads, oh, off with their heads
          –

ALICIA:    Whose heads, Alice? there's nobody here.

ALICE:    No, there never is, I'm all alone!

ALICIA:    What do you mean?

ALICE:    Nobody will play with me, nobody likes me!

*Gently ALICIA takes the red carpet and the cake-tin off her.
Underneath she still has the blue dress*

ALICIA:    Come, there there, it's no use crying like
          that, look at you, you're Alice, you've had a
          bad day, that's all –

ALICE:    A bad day? A bad week, a bad term, a bad
          *year*, Leesha, everybody hates me, I don't
          have any friends at all!

ALICIA:    But you've only been gone a few hours –

ALICE:    I've been here forever!

*Pause*

ALICIA:    I – think you've had a bad dream, dear,
          and everything about the new school that
          was frightening you – came true. You see
          I'm Alice too, deep down, only now I'm
          also *Alicia* and I understand most things.
          You wanted to be Queen so you were nasty

75

to *everybody* so now you have no friends.
You thought school would be horrid so you
dreamed about a horrid school!

ALICE:    *Then why are we still here?*

*It's getting darker*

ALICIA:    I – don't know, Alice, I don't quite know
that, but I'm thinking of the answer, and
thinking always solves things.

ALICE:    It comes every night, it starts with the
noises…

ALICIA:    What noises?

*Noises*

ALICIA:    *Oh!*

ALICE:    And then come the faces…

ALICIA:    What faces?

*Faces*

ALICIA:    *Oh!* Be off with you! You are only ill-
ucinations, you know!

ALICE:    So why are you talking to them, Leesha?

ALICIA:    I – don't quite know that either.

ALICE:    It comes at the end of the day, it knows we're
here.

ALICIA:    I'm not here, I'm safely in bed in England!

ALICE:    It all goes dark and I wake up alone,
screaming *Off with your head!* And no one will
play with me…

ALICIA:    Alice, we have to think…

ALICE:    I don't know how to think!

ALICIA:    Then let *me* think… If it always comes and
you always wake up, then it never really
hurts you, and if it never really hurts you, it
must be a sort of fiction and not real at all….

| | |
|---|---|
| ALICE: | But it's frightening, Leesha! |
| ALICIA: | Yes, yes, I'm frightened too, dear, so let's – tell the story of it, like you made all the stories here – like Once upon a time! Begin the story somewhere, what time of day is it, the light and dark time, I've forgotten what it's called, what is it? |
| ALICE: | It's brillig. |
| ALICIA: | Pardon? |
| ALICE: | It's brillig. |
| ALICIA: | There's no such word. |
| ALICE: | When all the twinkling lights come on. |
| ALICIA: | All right, but try and use words from the dictionary, Alice. It's brillig. No – it *was* brillig – then it's *just* like a story, and we lived to tell the tale! 'Twas brillig... Now the noises, and the faces – describe them! |
| ALICE: | *'Twas brillig, and the – slithy toves –* |
| ALICIA: | The what? |
| ALICE: | *Did gyre and gimble in the wabe...* |
| ALICIA: | Those aren't things one *does*, Alice! |
| ALICE: | *All mimsy were the borogoves*<br>*And the mome raths outgrabe...* |
| ALICIA: | But – yes, that's – actually... I'm not so scared now. You're good at this, Alice! |
| ALICE: | I am? |
| ALICIA: | It's your special power! I'm sure *I* couldn't do it. |
| ALICE: | Truly? |
| ALICIA: | You thought of the funny words and now there's nothing to be afraid of – |

*There is now: the CREATURE comes. They scream*

77

| | |
|---|---|
| ALICIA: | What is it? What's – the silliest name we can think of – *Fahrenheit!* |
| ALICE: | *Tweedledee!* |
| ALICIA: | *Vovolong!* |
| ALICE: | *JABBERWOCK!* |
| JAB'WOCK: | *JABBERWOCK!!!* |
| ALICE: | *Beware the Jabberwock, my dear!*<br>*The jaws that bite, the claws that catch!* |
| ALICIA: | What's *that?* |
| ALICE: | A Jubjub Bird! |
| ALICIA: | *Beware the Jubjub Bird!* Be off with you! |
| ALICE: | *And shun the – frumious Bandersnatch!* |
| ALICIA: | Get away! |

*The JABBERWOCK prepares to attack ALICIA*

| | |
|---|---|
| ALICIA: | It's looking at me, Alice, do something! |
| ALICE: | Take this, Leesha, it's a magic sword! |
| ALICIA: | There's nothing there! |
| ALICE: | *She took her – vorpal sword in hand –* |
| ALICIA: | Yes, I see it, it's vorpal, vorpal – |
| ALICE: | *Long time the – manxome foe she sought…* |
| ALICIA: | Yes it's manxome, so very manxome you are! |

*ALICIA and the JABBERWOCK circle each other*

| | |
|---|---|
| ALICE: | *So rested she by the Tum-Tum tree –* |
| ALICIA: | There isn't time, Alice, I'm ready, I'm ready! |
| ALICE: | Yes, the – the –<br>*The Jabberwock, with eyes of flame,*<br>*Came whiffling through the tulgey wood,*<br>*And burbled as it came!* |

*The JABBERWOCK swoops, burbling*

CREATURE: *JABBERWOCKY!!!*

ALICE/ALICIA: *LET MY SISTER BE!!!*

*They run it through. The JABBERWOCK collapses into fragments*

*ALICE and ALICIA dance for joy*

ALICE: *And hast thou slain the Jabberwock?*

ALICIA: *Come to my arms!*

ALICE: *My beamish girl!*
*Oh frabjous day! Calloo! Callay!*

*The fragments of the JABBERWOCK sing and dance*

ALICIA: Look at it now, it's turned into lots of different creatures…

ALICE: *The vorpal blade went snicker-snack!*

ALICIA: They don't look so frightening now, dear. And they're waving to you, look, like they want you to follow them.

ALICE: Oh I can do that *any* time.

ALICIA: You can?

ALICE: Yes every day there's a different story.

ALICIA: But then the Creature comes.

ALICE: At the end.

ALICIA: But you won't be afraid of it now, will you?

ALICE: Maybe at first, Leesha, but then I'll remember it's only a Jabberwock, and it always comes when it's brillig!

*Twas brillig and the slithy toves,*
*Did gyre and gimble in the wabe –*

ALICIA: Dear Alice. Do you think we might let Time – pass again?

ALICE: Why?

ALICIA: Perhaps Time – perhaps Time – *likes to pass.*

ALICE:      Oh. All right. Yes, perhaps it's lonely standing still, all on its own. As long as we can always play, and you have all the good ideas and I'll make up the stories!

ALICIA:      Come on then, little Alice.

ALICE:      I'm not *little*, Leesha!

ALICIA:      And I'm not Leesha…

*ALICIA holds out a hand for ALICE to take, and they make the Clasp together. ALICE looks into the distance the opposite way*

ALICE:      Look: what are those lights in the distance? I don't remember them, Leesha. Let's make a whole new story about them, it could be a magic castle!

ALICIA:      No. They're an old story, Alice. They're the lights of home. That's our bedroom. That's Lory's on the left, it's dark because she's away. And that's Edie's at the top, it's dark because she's asleep.

ALICE:      And that's mummy's on the right, all lit up inside!

ALICIA:      She must be very worried and sad.

ALICE:      When we go back, Leesha, I'll be like Edie, won't I, like a little sister to you, and you'll be like Lory to me, like an older sister, won't you, and won't it be nice to be four of us at Christmas! that's more presents to get, isn't it, but it's also more presents to give as well, it will all take much more gold and silver paper! And turkey, and fruit-cake, and mince pies, an *awful* lot of mince pies!

ALICIA:      Alice.

ALICE:      And we can always come back here, can't we? Sometimes be here, and sometimes be there, and I'll show you all around, and introduce you properly, how d'ye do and

shake hands, and we'll tell all the stories
there ever were!

| | |
|---|---|
| ALICIA: | Alice. |
| ALICE: | What's the matter? |

*ALICE understands*

| | |
|---|---|
| ALICE: | I – can't come back with you, can I. …That's all right. I – I like it here. And you'll always be welcome here, Leesha, I'll make sure of that! …You *will* be, you know. I mean you would be. Or, you would have been… Leesha? |
| ALICIA: | Yes, Alice? |
| ALICE: | Last time we parted, when I ran down the rabbit-hole, I did get very scared, you know. |
| ALICIA: | Yes, and I got very poorly, I had a temperature of 112. |
| ALICE: | Won't that happen to us again? If we part? |
| ALICIA: | I don't think so, Alice. Because I – don't think we're parting. |
| ALICE: | Oh… no I don't think so either. |
| ALICIA: | Not now Time is passing again. I've got to start at my new school tomorrow. I can't remember what I was scared of. |
| ALICE: | I'm off to a midnight feast! That's the next story, you know. I don't think I'll be the Red Queen again *ever*. No one wants to play with her. Do you think you'll be the White Queen again? No one likes her either, Leesha, she thinks she knows everything! |
| ALICIA: | No, Alice. She doesn't know very much at all, and I shan't be her again. |
| ALICE: | First I'm going to tell mummy how we beat the Jabberwock! |

*Pause*

| | |
|---|---|
| ALICIA: | Alice… |
| ALICE: | Yes, Leesha? |
| ALICIA: | Where will you – *find* mummy… |
| ALICE: | Oh she's everywhere. Some days she's in the kitchen cooking, and she gets so very bossy. Sometimes she's a Lion or a White Knight or a Mouse, but other days she's the Cat and she's almost like my best friend. |
| ALICIA: | Of course she is. |
| ALICE: | But you're my *actual* best friend, Leesha, we're best friends forever! |
| ALICIA: | And what's our favourite game? |
| ALICE/ALICIA: | *HIDE AND SEEK!* |
| ALICIA: | You hide, I'll seek. But when I find you I've won and then it's over… |
| ALICE: | But if you don't find me *I've* won and then it's over… |
| ALICIA: | But I'd keep on seeking so it wouldn't be over… |
| ALICE: | And I'd keep on hiding and you'd seek me forever… |
| ALICIA: | You'd be lonely though if no one ever found you… |
| ALICE: | No I wouldn't. There'd be all sorts of creatures and we'd all have won the game! |
| ALICIA: | Yes, my dear. You would all have won the game… |

*They part. ALICE for some twinkling coloured lanterns in the trees, ALICIA for the lights of home*

## 5 – ONCE UPON A TIME

*Christmas-time. The* COMPANY *sing a Christmas Carol*

*ALICIA's bedroom at home, hung with fairy-lights and cards. ALICIA runs in, home from her first term, in the smart black uniform. She is excitedly clutching a gift-wrapped present. Her* MOTHER *follows*

ALICIA:     Can I really open it now? but it's only Christmas Eve!

MOTHER:     You can open it now, dear.

ALICIA:     I'll call it an *un*-Christmas present!

MOTHER:     It's a present for a wonderful first term at school.

*ALICIA opens the present: it's a book*

ALICIA:     It's a book, it's a book, have I read it? I've –

*She opens the book and finds it blank*

ALICIA:     It's got no – it's got no title, and there's nothing – there's nothing inside, mum, it's blank…

MOTHER:     Oh no! You're absolutely right. I don't believe it. That is *so* disappointing. I'm going straight back to that bookshop and demanding my money back. Tuh! An empty book! Blank pages! Whoever thought of such a thing?

*ALICIA doesn't get the joke at first, then she slowly cottons on*

ALICIA:     It's – is it? – it's a book for me to write in…

MOTHER:     Well, I suppose you'd better get started, hadn't you? You've got no choice if there's nothing inside… I'd better leave you to it. Merry un-Christmas, dear.

*MOTHER goes. ALICIA is too excited to notice. She opens the book at the first page, and solemnly writes her name*

ALICIA:     *Hide and Seek, a Story. By Alicia Liddell.*

*She crosses that out and ponders a new name*

ALICIA:          *By Alibi…Anderson. Chapter One. Once upon a*
*time, there was a little girl who didn't know her*
*name…*

*ALICE appears, in the blue dress, watching her. ALICIA goes on writing*

ALICE:          Leesha. … Leesha?

*ALICIA turns as if she felt something in the air – but she can't see*
*ALICE any more*

ALICIA:          Edie? Was that you?

ALICE:          It's me, Leesha, it's Alice.

*Or hear her. ALICIA gets up from her desk and walks right past ALICE*
*as if she wasn't there*

ALICIA:          Mum?

*She shrugs and returns to her story, scribbling away. ALICE sighs*
*forlornly, downcast, and turns to go*

*Suddenly, in an instant, the WONDERLAND CREATURES come from*
*everywhere to encircle her – the WHITE RABBIT, the HATTER, the*
*HARE, the DORMOUSE, a bandaged HUMPTY-DUMPTY, TIGER-LILY*
*and VIOLET, TWEEDLEDUM, TWEEDLEDEE, and the smiling face*
*of the CHESHIRE CAT. They greet her like their best friend, all is*
*delight*

*They begin to move off cheerfully together, ALICE leaving last, with a*
*wave of farewell to the oblivious ALICIA – and then they're gone*

*ALICIA works on by the glow of the Christmas fairy-lights. We hear,*
*faraway, the WONDERLAND VOICES all echoing and mingling, the*
*catch-phrases of every character*

*And then the voices fade. ALICIA turns to the empty room, and gazes at*
*the spot where Alice had stood. She waves goodbye to where she was.*

*Then she carries on writing her story*

*Slow fade to darkness*

*          *          *

WIND IN THE WILLOWS

adapted for the stage by Glyn Maxwell
from the book by Kenneth Grahame

*for Anna Leader*

# Dramatis Personae

MOLE

RATTY

TOAD

BADGER

WEASEL

RUBY THE GAOLER'S DAUGHTER

THE SEA RAT

WOOLPACK THE JUDGE

COPPITT THE CONSTABLE

BOXALL THE GAOLER

DORIS THE WASHERWOMAN

BESS THE BARGEWOMAN

LEAST,

BLETT, &

VENKY, THE WEASELS

POOL,

SIP, &

FINICAL, THE FERRETS

HOB,

JILL, &

ERVIN, THE STOATS

BIRDS

WASHERWOMEN

*Wind in the Willows* was first performed on 11 July 2015 in the Open Air Theatre at Grosvenor Park, Chester, as part of the sixth summer season produced by Chester Performs. The play was staged in repertory with *Romeo and Juliet* and *The Merry Wives of Windsor* by William Shakespeare.

Glyn Maxwell's previous plays for the Grosvenor Park Open Air Theatre were *Merlin and the Woods of Time* (2011), *Masters Are You Mad?* (2012), and *Cyrano De Bergerac* (2013).

### Cast

Ellie Burrow – BESS, SIP
Jessica Clark – ERVIN, WOOLPACK
Tom Connor – JILL, COPPITT
Emilio Doorgasingh – LEAST
Daniel Goode – TOAD
Adam Harley – POOL, THE SEA RAT
Danielle Henry – HOB
James Holmes – BLETT, BOXALL
Adam Keast – RATTY
Louise Kempton – RUBY, FINICAL
Graham O'Mara – WEASEL
Sarah Quist – BADGER
Thomas Richardson – DORIS
Alix Ross – MOLE
Louise Shuttleworth – VENKY

### Creative Team

Alex Clifton – Director
Jessica Curtis – Designer
Harry Blake – Composer
Lee Proud – Choreographer
Philip D'Orleans – Fight Director
Rafaella Marcus – Assistant Director
Antonella Petraccaro – Costume Supervisor
Kay Magson – Casting

### Stage Management Team

Helen Keast – Stage Manager
Natalie James-Fox – Deputy Stage Manager
Tracey Booth, Amy Clarke – Assistant Stage Managers

### For Chester Performs

Andrew Bentley – Chief Executive Officer
Alex Clifton – Artistic Director
Amber Knipe – Head of Operations

# ACT ONE

*The BIRDS sing. MOLE emerges, covered in dust and whitewash*

MOLE:     Oh bother, oh blow, oh *hang* spring-cleaning!
          I'm going to take a break, I'm going to get
          some fresh air, I'm going to – *[Sniffs]* oh!
          It's summer. It's not spring it's summer.
          What a long time I've been down there…
          I've been keeping it very tidy! Mam and
          Dad said they won't be long… Bird-song,
          oh, like a Christmas carol in summer, why
          not sing carols in summer? *[Sniffs]* and oh,
          *small creatures* are hereabouts, close by…
          Oh it's *not* a day for cleaning. Perhaps it's
          a day for nothing I expected. I'm going to
          have a – a – a *day off!* A – *holiday!* Well, here
          I go, I'd better, oh. What does one *do* on a
          Day Off? I don't know. Perhaps I'll look at
          all the creatures having a Day *On…* She's
          busy doing her job: her job must be to sit
          there eating, she does it very well. And *his*
          job must be to be holding that drink for
          someone who'll need it later. Mustn't break
          his concentration. What funny jobs creatures
          have. Oh. I've been walking again. Home is
          *this* way, I'm sure, not that way, never go that
          way, I –

*The roar of a Digger nearby! MOLE cowers till it stops*

MOLE:     Oh my, oh my, they said they won't be
          long…

*She looks at the picture of her parents*

MOLE:     Home is oh, home is where, was it this way?
          That way? The birds would tell me but
          they've flown away and something in the air
          doesn't care any more!

*Whispering in the bushes*

MOLE:          What was that? Who's there? Oh! Which way's home, which way? Oh my, I've lost my way!

*MOLE runs off. THREE STOATS – HOB, JILL and ERVIN – emerge from the bushes*

HOB:          That was funny, she can't see well!

JILL:          Cool! We can, she can't, she just goes *sniffsniffsniff…*

ERVIN:        Guys, guys –

HOB:          She was scared of the big scary noise!

JILL:          She was! We weren't! *Sniffsniffsniff…*

ERVIN:        Guys, guys, thing is, I *was* – a bit. No no no no listen I was just like a *tiny* bit scared of the big scary noise.

HOB:          /Ha ha ha! yeah I was.

JILL:          /Ha ha ha! a little bit yeah.

ERVIN:        What do you think it was, guys.

HOB/JILL:    Big./Scary.

HOB:          And noisy, like a – like a big scary noise.

ERVIN:        I wanna go home.

HOB:          No you *don't*. Home's all like *parents*.

ERVIN:        We're s'posed to be at school.

HOB:          *Ssshhh!*

JILL:          School's all like *teachers*.

ERVIN:        But they might know what the big scary noise was!

*WEASEL emerges from the crowd*

WEASEL:      Well I just might be able to help you there, lads…

HOB:          Who are you, mister?

| | |
|---|---|
| JILL: | You ain't one of us. |
| WEASEL: | Oh I think you'll find we're *all* one of us. |
| JILL/HOB: | Eh?/Wot? |
| ERVIN: | Mister, do *you* know what made the big scary noise? |
| WEASEL: | Know it? Why it's a very good friend of mine. You can meet it if you like. Wouldn't be so big and scary then, would it. |
| HOB: | We can – meet it? |
| WEASEL: | Well yes, if you join the Gang. Look, badges… |
| HOB: | I wanna join the Gang. |
| JILL: | I'm joining if you are! |
| ERVIN: | You tryin' to leave me out of things again? |
| WEASEL: | How about you tag along with me, little stoats, and be big and scary too? |
| HOB: | I'm in. (I'm big already.) |
| JILL: | Me too. (Been told I'm scary.) |
| ERVIN: | I've got a badge. |

*WEASEL leads the STOATS away*

*The Riverbank. The BIRDS, drawn by the lovely sounds, return and make RATTY's home. RATTY dozes in a chair…*

| | |
|---|---|
| RATTY: | *You know it isn't time to be thinking of going… if you've got to leave this place and your brother who'll miss you… couldn't you stay here just this once? You've no idea what good times we have while you're far away…* |

*MOLE stumbles in and RATTY wakes*

| | |
|---|---|
| RATTY: | Oh I say! |
| MOLE: | Oh my! |
| RATTY: | Oh I say… |
| MOLE: | Oh my oh my… |

RATTY:      We could keep this up all day, couldn't we, old chap, but if you're going to drop in on the old homestead I'd sooner know your name…

MOLE:       I'm, I'm – Moley.

RATTY:      And I'm the Water-Rat, and *this* is the River-Bank.

MOLE:       Oh my, you *live* – by the *river*?

RATTY:      By it, with it, on it and in it. It's brother and sister to me, food and drink and company and I wouldn't want no other.

MOLE:       But isn't it a bit – lonely at times? Just you and the river and no one to talk to?

RATTY:      You're not from round here, are you.

MOLE:       No, my home is that way. Or – *that* way? (oh my!)

RATTY:      When I meet a little fellow who's not from round here, I want to show that fellow what a fine place we dwell in, and what a cracking life we lead! Lonely? Quiet? With the birds and the otters and the dabchicks and moorhens, and the rabbits (they're all right) and the squirrels (if you like that sort of thing) anyway it's brunches, lunches, picnics and suppers from daylight to moonlight and back again, you just caught us all snoozing our lunch off, that's all!

MOLE:       Oh, it's all so very different… you see *my* comfy chair goes *there*, and my fireplace goes right *there*, and my table –

RATTY:      Not every day I see one of you lot running out of the Wood like that. Thought you folks were sworn under-grounders.

MOLE:       Well I'm – I'm having a day off, you see, doing a bit of exploring, yes! No as soon as I

|            | want to go home, oh, I'll just stroll off along that way… (or *that* way? or *that*? oh my…) |
|------------|---|
| RATTY:     | The Wild Wood's not much fun these days, you know. We river-bankers never go there by ourselves. |
| MOLE:      | (I wonder if he can help me get home…) |
| RATTY:     | Been hearing some nasty rumours, loud noises no one's heard before… |
| MOLE:      | Mr Water-Rat, sir – |
| RATTY:     | Just 'Ratty', if you wouldn't mind. |
| MOLE:      | Mr Ratty sir, I'm afraid I have to – |
| RATTY:     | Now, since you're here, and you're honouring the old homestead with a visit, what say we pack ourselves a picnic and head out on the river eh? |
| MOLE:      | (Oh I want to go home) but I was wondering if, if – |
| RATTY:     | It's such a perfect day for a picnic no? |
| MOLE:      | Oh yes but – |
| RATTY:     | Will you help me pack the old hamper? |
| MOLE:      | Oh yes, Mr Ratty, of course, but – |

*RATTY starts packing a hamper*

|            |   |
|------------|---|
| RATTY:     | But what, my dear fellow (cold chicken cold tongue cold ham cold beef…) |
| MOLE:      | I can't, I can't – |
| RATTY:     | Ye-es, what *can't* you do (lots of fruit, and a little cake…) |
| MOLE:      | I don't know how to – |
| RATTY:     | (Actually lots of cake, and a little fruit…) |
| MOLE:      | I don't know how to – 'head out on the river!' |
| RATTY:     | What's that? |

MOLE:    I don't know how to swim!

RATTY:   Bless my soul we don't swim in it, you know.
         We take the boat of course! Lend a hand eh,
         there's a good fellow.

*RATTY gets his boat out, MOLE helps*

MOLE:    I – I – I've never been in a boat before.

RATTY:   What? Never been? What *have* you been
         doing...

MOLE:    I've been tidying (they won't be long) is it –
         nice to be in a boat?

RATTY:   Nice? It's the only thing! Believe me, my
         good fellow, there's nothing, *absolutely*
         nothing, half so much worth doing as simply
         messing about in boats...

MOLE:    Messing about, in boats, I – I don't know –

RATTY:   Nothing seems to matter, that's the charm of
         it. Whether you go to the edge of somewhere
         or the middle of nowhere, halfway to the
         horizon or all the way to right back here, it's
         up to you, it's your beeswax, your boat, your
         afternoon! Climb aboard, eh, ya landlubber!

*They get in, and the BIRDS take it out on the River*

MOLE:    Oh my, oh my! We're *on* – the River...

RATTY:   Winter or summer, autumn or spring, it's
         always got its fun, its excitements. What the
         river hasn't got is not worth having, and what
         the river doesn't know is not worth knowing.

MOLE:    Then it knows my way home!

RATTY:   I'm – sure it does.

MOLE:    Not that *I* don't know, *I* know my way home!
         (oh my)

RATTY:   I'm sure you do, now just sit back and enjoy
         yourself...

| | |
|---|---|
| MOLE: | Yes Ratty, all right Ratty. Ratty… |
| RATTY: | Ye-es… |
| MOLE: | What's beyond the Wild Wood? I don't see very well, it seems like clouds that stand too still for clouds, hills that stand too tall for hills, and all that smoke, and clanking! |
| RATTY: | Never mind all that. That's just the Wide World, and the less said the better. |
| MOLE: | It just it seems – they seem – to be always getting bigger… Or am I always getting smaller? |
| RATTY: | You know what I'm getting, Moley? Hungrier and thirstier! We've been on the river a good three minutes, what say we unpack the supplies eh? |
| MOLE: | Oh yes, oh yes, oh yes! |

*RATTY and MOLE enjoy their picnic for a moment, till the loud annoying noise of an engine scatters the BIRDS and the boat capsizes. RATTY and MOLE soaked, RATTY pulling MOLE to shore. Enter TOAD, in his speedboat. RATTY protests about the noise, but his voice is drowned out*

| | |
|---|---|
| TOAD: | SORRY, RATSTER, WHAT D'YOU SAY THERE? NOISE, WHAT NOISE? NOT MAKING SENSE, OLD MAN, LET ME SWITCH OFF THE OLD CHUG-A-CHUG, there, that's better… |

*Sudden quiet except for RATTY*

| | |
|---|---|
| RATTY: | *– that blasted thing off!* |
| TOAD: | Pipe down, Ratty, place of beauty and all that. |
| RATTY: | It *was,* it *was,* until you – spoiled it with this – *monster!* |
| TOAD: | Monster ain't she just! Teak interior, fuel-injected engine, forty mph, I call her *Princess* |

|          | *Toad*, what d'you think, Ratster? – who's this little feller? |
|----------|----------------------------------------------------------------|
| MOLE:    | Hehehe I'm – |
| RATTY:   | My friend Mole and I were having a peaceful row on the river, Toad, when you – |
| TOAD:    | It *is* peaceful, isn't it, spot on, it makes you just want to shout out I AM AT PEACE! THE TOAD IS NOW AT PEACE! and you know, Ratster, the *Princess* here can do forty mph top whack, which means I can zoom to *any* peaceful spot *five hundred per cent* faster than I did in days of yore! (Ooh are those fondant-fancies…) |
| RATTY:   | What happened to your rowing-boat, Toad, I helped you pick it out, I taught you to row it. |
| TOAD:    | *[Eating]* Well you know, Ratterton (pink icing *yesss*) the thing about that rowing-boat *is*, that you have to flipping well *row* it! I thought a rowing-boat was *a boat that rowed!* Well it bloomin' well don't. Between you and me and this quiet feller here it just sits there bobbing like some big, silly, cork on the river! |
| RATTY:   | Oh good lord, truly I give up. |
| MOLE:    | Hello, Mr Toad,/my name is Moley – |
| TOAD:    | /Did the salesman tell me I had to row it myself? No, he did not. Scoundrel. There. That's that said. I hereby take this fondant-fancy, for to Soothe My Feelings. *[Eating]* Not soothed… almost soothed… soothed. Well, now I have a *speedboat* and it is precisely what it says it is – a boat that goes at speed! |
| RATTY:   | *Why don't you stay where you are?* |
| TOAD:    | What's that, old boy? (ooh, *yellow* icing…) |

| | |
|---|---|
| RATTY: | You have a splendid house in sumptuous grounds, for heaven's sake. Why don't you try standing still one day and looking around at how – *lovely* it all is, and, and, – |
| TOAD: | And what, old man? |
| RATTY: | And nothing! |
| TOAD: | Nothing? What's the point of that? No, look at this, it's my checklist of beauty-spots I've chalked off today. I am *doing Beauty*, Ratster, and I feel like a millionaire! |
| RATTY: | You *are* a millionaire. Or you were. |
| TOAD: | Million here, million there, what's money when there's *beauty* to be had? |
| RATTY: | Sit down, Toad, stop being an ass, this is madness even by *your* high standards – |
| TOAD: | Can't do it, Ratster, got a date with a willow-tree where some young lovers (*eeuuww*) are *holding hands* (*eeuuww*) it's a beauty-spot, it's on my list, collect the set, can't waste time talking! |

*TOAD roars away in his speedboat. RATTY groans*

| | |
|---|---|
| MOLE: | Oh my. He's not at peace at all! |
| RATTY: | Once upon a time he loved a canary-coloured cart. Before that he sang ballads to the glory of his bicycle. |
| MOLE: | But he's spoiling the place, Ratty, your lovely river-bank. *And* he took the last fondant-fancy. |
| RATTY: | He did? Maybe you're right. He really has gone too far this time. Time we took a stand, eh? |
| MOLE: | *We?* oh. *We...* Because, well, I should probably be heading home soon and all that... |

| | |
|---|---|
| RATTY: | Oh… |
| MOLE: | Sort of thing… |
| RATTY: | No of course… |
| MOLE: | Time getting on… |
| RATTY: | Quite so, quite so… |

*RATTY looks so sad. MOLE sighs*

| | |
|---|---|
| MOLE: | But I could help you for a *short* while, if – |
| RATTY: | You know I wouldn't mind that, Moley – |
| MOLE: | Just until we set him straight – |
| RATTY: | For the Riverbank, eh? |
| MOLE: | For the Riverbank! Hm. Hooray! |
| RATTY: | Now let's get some dry clothes on. I know where we have to go. She always knows what's best. |
| MOLE: | She? A friend on the Riverbank, is she, a neighbour of yours? |
| RATTY: | Oh no. The personage to whom I refer lives deep in the heart of the Wild Wood. |
| MOLE: | The – oh I see – deep in the (oh my)… |
| RATTY: | Let's go and rustle up some dry things, and vital supplies for the journey. |
| MOLE: | Oh, biscuits and jam and fondant-fancies and that? |
| RATTY: | I mean pistols and sticks and a map and a compass! |

*RATTY goes. MOLE looks at the photo of her parents*

| | |
|---|---|
| MOLE: | Oh? good, very good, yes, pistols, sticks, oh my. I wish I never left the – but I did make a friend, and I did row on a River…oh my. But I *came* through the Wild Wood, it must be *near* the Wild Wood. And Ratty says there's a personage who always knows best. Perhaps |

the personage knows where my home is.
Pistols and sticks oh my!

*MOLE hurries off after RATTY. The BIRDS remove RATTY's place
and then are driven away by the sound of the Digger again. THREE
FERRETS – POOL, SIP and FINICAL (with a clipboard) – hurry away
from it. The Digger stops and they look back at it*

POOL:  I call it the Screaming Yellow Dragon.

SIP:  Ooh, that's good, are we calling it that officially?

FINICAL:  *[Reading]* Hmm, we've not voted on a name-change.

POOL:  It's a nickname. Best thing to do when something starts wiping out your homes is to give it a nickname.

SIP:  I don't think it's *all* our homes, actually, it's about 60% is it?

FINICAL:  *[Reading]* Um, 63% destroyed, 22% uninhabitable.

SIP:  Funny that word, 'uninhabitable' because you'd think '*in*-habitable' would be the negative, as in 'not habitable', no?

FINICAL:  Look are we voting on the name-change?

POOL:  Screaming Yellow Dragon.

FINICAL:  *[Reading]* Other nominations are: Earth-Shifter From Hell (which I quite like)...

SIP:  That was mine.

FINICAL:  ...and – where is it – oh yes, Homeless-Maker.

SIP:  Homeless, where?

POOL:  It refers to *us*. Making *us* homeless.

SIP:  Oh. Could we maybe *not* call it that?

FINICAL:  Look, team, we've slightly gone off-piste, we're supposed to be organizing A-Com.

| | |
|---|---|
| POOL: | A-Com? |
| FINICAL: | Apocalypse Committee. |
| SIP: | Oh I was thinking for A-Com an *informal* sort of atmosphere, smart casual? around a table but with a side-buffet for nibbles and dips and so on… |
| FINICAL: | Shouldn't take more than an hour, just checking the Agenda… Welcome from the Chairperson, Apologies for Absence, Matters Arising, Likely Extinction of *Mustela Putorius*, Buffet Rota, Date of Next Meeting – |
| POOL: | Wait wait, go back one – |
| FINICAL: | Um, Buffet Rota – yes we need to talk about taramasalata – |
| POOL: | No, back another one – |
| FINICAL: | Um, Likely Extinction of *Mustela Putorius* – |
| POOL: | Yes that one, what's that when it's at home? |
| SIP: | Oh let's leave that to the experts! |
| FINICAL: | It means *ferret*, it's us, it's our Latin name, thus, Likely Extinction of *Ferrets*. |
| POOL: | Ah…gotcha. |
| FINICAL: | *Then* comes Buffet Rota, and the taramasalata issue. |
| SIP: | We've got a Latin name, we're official, *get in there!* |
| POOL: | I'd like to propose that we/abolish all Latin nomenclature – |
| FINICAL: | /That's a matter for the Proposal Committee/ which meets – |
| SIP: | /On which I'll have you know I'm the chair! You should make friends with me, eh? |
| WEASEL: | *I* think you should all make friends with *me*. |

*WEASEL comes*

| | |
|---|---|
| POOL: | Who might you be? |
| FINICAL: | You're not *Mustela Putorius.* |
| WEASEL: | No no. I'm *Mustela Nivalis.* |
| SIP: | Hm, that *is* kind of a cooler name, guys? |
| FINICAL: | *[Reading]* I don't see you on the schedule… |
| WEASEL: | Oh I'm digital, contactless, clean, I'm in the Cloud. |
| POOL/SIP: | Huh the Cloud! |
| WEASEL: | *[To FINICAL]* Ah I do love your sweet little scraps of paper, very old-school, my friend! |

*POOL and SIP laugh. Embarrassed, FINICAL tears up his agenda*

| | |
|---|---|
| WEASEL: | Now I can see you're worried about recent changes in the Wild Wood. Wouldn't you like to invest in a scheme that will protect you in the future? We at WeaselCo understand your hopes and fears. |
| POOL: | *Digital, clean, in the Cloud…* |
| SIP: | *Mustela nivalis…contactless…* |
| FINICAL: | What can you do about the Screaming Yellow Dragon? |
| WEASEL: | Who? Oh you mean Slurpex? Slurpex is a private entity working in association with WeaselCo. You as shareholders in the Conglomerate would also have a stake in Slurpex (terms and conditions apply)… |
| SIP: | */ Stake in Slurpex… Nivalis…* |
| POOL: | */ Conglomerate…in the Cloud…* |
| FINICAL: | */ Terms and conditions apply…* |
| WEASEL: | This can all be yours if you buy a stake… This catalogue here is the glossiest one published *since records began…* |

FERRETS:          *WeaselCo...Slurpex...Nivalis...*

*WEASEL produces the catalogue. The FERRETS pore over and leaf and sniff the pages*

WEASEL:          *[To FINICAL]* Now *you* look like you might be able to stretch to *Platinum* membership, which comes with a shiny card...

FINICAL:          How shiny?

*WEASEL gives him a platinum card*

WEASEL:          You can see your face in it.

FINICAL:          This is *your* face.

WEASEL:          Close enough. Shall we go?

*WEASEL leads the FERRETS away*

*RATTY and MOLE come cautiously into the Wild Wood with rucksacks. RATTY reads his map and compass irritably. MOLE sniffs the air, shakes her head sadly*

MOLE:          It smells – dark.

RATTY:          I can see it's dark (east? no north...)

MOLE:          This isn't the way.

RATTY:          No? Well it's *one* way, I'm just trying to see *which* way.

MOLE:          It isn't the way I came.

RATTY:          Is it not, well that's interesting, but what we're looking for is the way we're *going*, not the way you came, all right?

MOLE:          I was only saying... *[Sniffs]* I think some ferrets were here just now.

RATTY:          Really, not my type (help me, stars, that's due north...)

MOLE:          I wish I'd never...

RATTY:          What's that now?

MOLE:          Nothing.

RATTY:     (North-west, or north-north-west...)

MOLE:      Oh, nothing smells the same as it did...

RATTY:     You see *that* way there should be trees, a
           lime-tree grove but there's nothing. It's as if
           the trees all just – went away. Well the map
           must be wrong that's all. Or old. Or new.

MOLE:      We should turn back to yours, Ratty, while
           we still can.

RATTY:     Not listening.

MOLE:      And it's getting truly dark.

RATTY:     Is it really, how *about* that.

MOLE:      I don't like it here, oh my.

RATTY:     Oh and I think it's delightful. Do be quiet,
           old chap, we're nowhere near where we need
           to be.

*MOLE can't hold back the tears. She sniffs. RATTY misunderstands*

RATTY:     That's better, Moley, keep sniffing the air,
           find out who dwells in this neck of the
           Wood...

MOLE:      Aye-aye cap'n.

RATTY:     Let me know if you smell something black
           and white and wise and bossy...

MOLE:      Mm-hm.

*RATTY glances, realizes MOLE is crying. He has no idea what to do, so
he folds up the map and makes a decision*

RATTY:     Right! Let's have some fun!

MOLE:      Fun, how...

RATTY:     Well, I've kept it a surprise, Moley, but this
           was the plan all along: we're on a camping
           trip!

MOLE:      Oh?

*RATTY empties the rucksacks*

| | |
|---|---|
| RATTY: | That's right! Always prepared! Sleeping-bags and snacks, thermos flasks and torches! Got things for a little fire here, heigh-ho, not so bad now, is it? Jump to it, help me out! |
| MOLE: | Oh yes, what fun! |
| RATTY: | We'll pretend we're back at home, eh? So the comfy chairs would go there, and there, |
| MOLE: | Yes yes, and Ratty, perhaps – |
| RATTY: | And the stove can go where the fireplace is – |
| MOLE: | In *my* home, the chairs are – |
| RATTY: | No, Moley, they go there, we're making it just like home! |
| MOLE: | (*Your* home maybe – ) |
| RATTY: | Now I suggest we hunker down for the night, and at first light we'll see precisely where we are. |
| MOLE: | Yes yes but can we – stay awake and tell stories, Ratty? |
| RATTY: | Well not really, old chap, I… Why yes, of course. What would a camping trip be without a couple of stories? |
| MOLE: | Hooray! Go on, you first, then me, then you again and so on through the night! |
| RATTY: | Through the night eh, I'm a little groggy for that, old chap… |
| MOLE: | Please, Ratty! |
| RATTY: | Oh all right. Through the night it is. |
| MOLE: | Go on, go on, you start! |
| RATTY: | Very well. |
| MOLE: | (*Yesss!*) |
| RATTY: | Now: once upon a time… |

| | |
|---|---|
| MOLE: | Yes Ratty? It's a good beginning, but then what happened? |
| RATTY: | Oh… once upon a time there was a, a sea rat, you see, not a water rat a sea rat, and he… *[Yawns]* went to see the sea… |
| MOLE: | Yes? Yes, and what happened when he went to the sea? |
| RATTY: | Went to see the sea… |
| MOLE: | Please don't fall asleep, Ratty, I'll be all alone, what *happens* to the sea rat? |
| RATTY: | To see… what he could see… |

*RATTY starts snoring, and MOLE is all alone*

| | |
|---|---|
| MOLE: | Ratty. Ratty? The story, Ratty… Oh my. |

*Hisses and sounds all around, an owl hooting, frightening MOLE, who starts rearranging everything to look like her home*

| | |
|---|---|
| MOLE: | Oh my – my turn. Once upon a time there was a Mole, and she lived in a house called Mole End which was the coziest house in the world! She kept her home very tidy, the comfy chair went here, and the fireplace was right *here*, and the special lamp was here, and – |

*Faraway, the sound of pan-pipes*

| | |
|---|---|
| MOLE: | Oh! That melody again… Mam and Dad used to say that was the god-of-little-creatures. He sings his song when he hears your heart beat, to show you *his* heart's beating too… oh thank you, little creature, sing your song, sing your song… |

*The pan-pipes play. MOLE falls asleep. RATTY stirs*

| | |
|---|---|
| RATTY: | *Brother…brother…where are you travelling now…* |

*In his dream he sees THE SEA RAT*

| | |
|---|---|
| SEA RAT: | The Grecian islands and the Adriatic, amber, rose and aquamarine… rode into Venice down a path of gold… |
| RATTY: | *You know it isn't time to be thinking of going…* |
| SEA RAT: | The Grand Canal at night, the air full of music, great stars set in a velvet sky…we sat late into the night, drinking with our friends… |
| RATTY: | *Have you got to go? Your brother will miss you…* |
| SEA RAT: | The little boats lie tethered to the old sea-wall… |
| RATTY: | *Couldn't you stay here just this once?* |
| SEA RAT: | The salmon leap on the flood-tide and you'll come too, young brother, for the days pass, and the South still waits for you… Take the adventure, heed the call! |

*The SEA RAT goes. RATTY wakes up alone. The pipes fade*

| | |
|---|---|
| RATTY: | Oh… That face again, and that song, that old minstrel of my dreams… Both gone now, heigh-ho. Alone in the Wood with Moley. Moley you awake? never mind. Bit of shut-eye, little fellow, that's the ticket. Alone in the Wood with Moley… |

*RATTY goes back to sleep. THREE WEASELS – LEAST, BLETT and VENKY – find them*

| | |
|---|---|
| LEAST: | Oi. Strangers at nine o'clock. |
| BLETT: | That's not for ages, mate. |
| LEAST: | I mean, their *position* is nine o'clock. |
| BLETT: | Nope. Lost me, mate. |
| VENKY: | That's a rat. Dunno what *that* is. |
| BLETT: | Ha! It's got glasses. Sweet. |
| VENKY: | Why are they here *together*? Don't like that one bit. |

| | |
|---|---|
| LEAST: | This is a river-dweller. This is an undergrounder. |
| BLETT: | *We're* undergrounders, mate. |
| LEAST: | Yeah but we're – y'know. |
| BLETT: | Weasels. Point taken. |
| VENKY: | Ssh. Right, we'll follow this one home. *[MOLE]* |
| LEAST: | Why? What's it got? |
| BLETT: | It's got glasses. Ha! Four-eyes. |
| VENKY: | Boss says find out all we can about who lives where. |
| LEAST: | We don't live anywhere, since that monster came – |
| VENKY: | Shut it. It's not a monster. The boss is on top of it. |
| LEAST: | That thing *works* for the boss? |
| VENKY: | Don't ask questions, search their bags for food. |
| BLETT: | I'm gonna swipe its glasses! |
| BADGER: | What do you think you're doing. |

*A stern voice from above. The BADGER, in her dressing-gown and slippers, holding a lantern*

| | |
|---|---|
| VENKY: | Nothing. None of your business. |
| BADGER: | What's done in this wood is my business. |
| LEAST: | Why's that then. |
| BADGER: | What's done in this world is my business. |
| LEAST: | Get you. They're trespassers. |
| BADGER: | How are they trespassers. |
| LEAST: | Cos they're – trespassing? In my book that makes 'em trespassers. |
| BADGER: | And are we all just pages in your book? |
| LEAST: | Er – |

| | |
|---|---|
| BADGER: | Is it *your* world we dwell in? |
| LEAST: | Well, no, not officially, but – |
| BADGER: | Then how is it your business? Do you live here? |
| LEAST: | Well not right *here*, but – |
| BADGER: | I do. Come with a good will or not at all. |
| VENKY: | Friends of yours, are they? |
| BADGER: | What would that matter. They are creatures in my sight, and you will let them be. |
| BLETT: | They – look at them, they don't *belong* here! |
| BADGER: | Time brought them here, they belong here quite as much as you or I. |
| BLETT: | We got friends, you know. |
| BADGER: | I'm delighted for you. Buy them ice cream. In the meantime *get out of my sight*. |

*Cowed, the WEASELS disperse. BADGER whistles and the BIRDS appear, making BADGER's home around the sleeping MOLE and RATTY*

| | |
|---|---|
| BADGER: | What's brought *you* here in the night, I wonder. |

*The pan-pipes again. BADGER listens*

| | |
|---|---|
| BADGER: | Again, there it is… Once upon a time that song had words, how did it go now… *Helper and healer, I cheer…small waifs in the woodland wet*…what was next… *You shall look on my power at the hopeless hour, but then you shall forget*… Hmm. *Then you shall forget*… Play on, old friend, play on, I'll be here when you call on me… |

*A cock crows, the pipes fade, the BIRDS fly. RATTY and MOLE wake up in BADGER's parlour, tucking into breakfast, the night forgotten*

| | |
|---|---|
| RATTY: | So I said to him, can't you stay still for just one moment? |

MOLE: But he was shouting *Peace! Peace! I'm the Toad and I'm at peace!* he's so funny!

RATTY: He's not remotely funny. Badger he's making a highway of the River-bank, and as for the state of his bank-balance, I rather dread to imagine.

BADGER: The whole inheritance is probably gone by now. What *would* his father have said…

RATTY: Old Rear-Admiral Toad? He'd be at his wit's end like me, old girl, what the blazes do we *do* with him? It's the worst he's ever been, he's a menace to himself!

BADGER: You, and I, and our new friend the Mole, shall take him seriously in hand. No nonsense. We shall bring him back to reason, by force if need be. We light out for Toad Hall directly after breakfast.

MOLE: Oh, but it's still breakfast for a while, yes? it's truly such a feast, Mrs Badger –

BADGER: Don't you worry, little snuffler, I assure you we are deep in the midst of breakfast.

MOLE: It's just it's so nice to be underground again!

BADGER: Only way to live, eh?

RATTY: Oh *very* nice I'm sure, no breezes, no birdsong, no windows, no view, what would you want with a view? oh *very* nice…

*RATTY stretches and starts reading the Wild Wood Chronicle*

MOLE: No but where *you* live, Ratty, is the only way to live when you're *there*, and where *you* live, Mrs Badger, is the only way to live now I'm *here*, and where Toad lives is the only way to live if you're Toad perhaps, but where *I* live, is, where was I –

BADGER: You make perfect sense to me.

| | |
|---|---|
| RATTY: | *[Reading] Yesss!* |
| MOLE: | Pardon? |
| BADGER: | What's up, Rat? |
| RATTY: | Field-mice bowled the Squirrels out for 90. Bravo, little fellers! |

*BADGER and MOLE exchange looks. No idea what he's on about*

| | |
|---|---|
| MOLE: | You know where you *are*, underground, nothing can hurt you, nothing can happen unless you decide it should do, you don't have to ask anyone can I do this or that please! |
| BADGER: | Exactly so. Underground it's peaceful, cool, and tranquil. And then if you wish to expand your ideas, why, you dig a little, scrape and scrooge and scrabble a little, and in no time you've dug yourself a whole new bedroom! No builders or tradesmen or neighbours making sly remarks over the fence. |
| RATTY | *[Reading]* Well I *like* having neighbours, even ones I can't stand. |
| MOLE: | Oh and you have your chair *there*, and your fireplace right *there*, and your bed's just waiting for you *there*, and when you need a snack you just walk over *here*, and, |
| BADGER: | And how far is *your* home from here, Mole? |
| MOLE: | The little lamp is *there*... Pardon? |
| BADGER: | Is it far away? Your home. |

*MOLE too homesick for words*

| | |
|---|---|
| RATTY: | *[Reading]* We'll find it, old chap. |
| BADGER: | That's right, you'll see it soon enough. When I was your age I left home for a long old time, I did, and I believe it did me the power of good. I wouldn't do it now, mind you, don't really have the legs for it, but for |

a youngster it might be just the right thing to go roaming faraway.

MOLE:     Faraway, oh yes, I'm sure, roaming, just the right thing… But your home is so *amazing*, how did you do it all?

RATTY:    Oh no, don't start her off…

BADGER:   It would indeed be amazing if I *had* done it all. But you know what, I *found* my home. Oh I've added things on here and there, as you do, but most of it was down here waiting for me. Empty chambers and passageways, they stretch for miles… I see I'll have to show you…

MOLE:     Yes please!

RATTY:    Oh here we go.

*BADGER starts to show MOLE round the place*

BADGER:   Long ago, on the spot where this Wild Wood now grows so dark and wondrous, there was a city of *People* here. Yes, *People*, they had a great city all to themselves. Sometimes I think I see them, as if they left their imprint. Right here where we're standing, they lived and walked and talked…

RATTY:    And messed about in boats…

BADGER:   …and undoubtedly messed about in boats, and did what People do. There are still some songs about them, but they all have the same chorus. How they built up very high, and when they'd filled up all the sky they dug down very low, as you see now all about you, and they feasted and fought and bargained and bettered and bested each other. They must have thought their city would last forever. They say there were badgers here long before that city came to

|  | be. Yes and moles too! And here we are again. We're an enduring lot. |
|---|---|
| MOLE: | There's all sorts of creatures in the Wood, aren't there Mrs Badger, when I taste the air I know they're all around me, but some are new and I don't know what they look like. |
| BADGER: | I'm afraid that *that*, Mole, is the *return* of People. |
| RATTY: | *[Reading]* Spoil her breakfast, why don't you. |
| BADGER: | She ought to know what's what. |
| MOLE: | I can hear the young ones talking sometimes... |
| BADGER: | Oh the young ones are our friends. |
| MOLE: | And the older ones? |
| BADGER: | We don't know. We're not even sure *they* do. But they're back, and that's for sure. If a certain Water Rat ever read anything but the sports pages he'd know there are shrews and stoats and ferrets, rabbits, weasels, squirrels, bats, roaming the Wood, homeless creatures, bitter little beasts, lost souls with bones to pick. There comes that great dark sound in the daytime, it screams and shudders and stops. |
| MOLE: | Oh I heard it it's so loud! |
| BADGER: | It's loud so we can't hear what it's doing. |
| MOLE: | What *is* it doing? |
| RATTY: | Steady, old girl, these are campfire stories. |
| MOLE: | *[To RATTY]* Oh and you know *all* about campfire stories. |
| RATTY: | What's that supposed to mean? |
| MOLE: | *[Mimicking RATTY]* Once upon a time there was a... |

*MOLE pretends to fall asleep and BADGER shrieks with laughter*

| | |
|---|---|
| RATTY: | Oh *highly* amusing. |
| BADGER: | Highly! |
| MOLE: | A sea rat went to see the sea! *[Snores]* |
| RATTY: | What's that? |
| MOLE: | To see what sea the rat could see! *[Snores]* |
| RATTY: | Is that what I said? Well. Nothing wrong with a sea rat, my friends, I've a brother who's a sea rat. Haven't seen him for years, poor beggar. Now *there's* a life I'd hate to lead… |
| BADGER: | You will dwell on that river-bank for as long as there's a river. |
| RATTY: | Oh, will I, will I really. |
| BADGER: | It would quite dry up if you left it, Rat. |
| RATTY: | No it wouldn't. One day I'll surprise you all. |
| BADGER: | Indeed. Now I think it's about time we paid a visit on a certain friend of ours… |

*BADGER whistles, the BIRDS dismantle Badger's place. The FRIENDS set off for Toad Hall. The Digger roars into life and the BIRDS scatter. WEASEL leads in his GANG, clicks his fingers and the Digger stops*

| | |
|---|---|
| WEASEL: | Do you know what that thing is? |
| GANG: | NO! |
| WEASEL: | Are you afraid of it? |
| GANG: | YES! |
| WEASEL: | Can you stop it if you want? |
| GANG: | NO! |
| WEASEL: | Can *I* stop it if I want? |
| GANG: | YES! |
| WEASEL: | *So are you WeaselCo!* |
| GANG: | YES! |

| | |
|---|---|
| ERVIN: | NO! (I mean YES, sorry, I keep doing that...) |
| WEASEL: | Did you lose your home, little stoat? |
| ERVIN: | Yeah... |
| WEASEL: | Would you like a home, little stoat? |
| ERVIN: | Yeah! |
| WEASEL: | So. *Are you WeaselCo?* |
| ERVIN: | Eh? we done that one already. |

*WEASEL hisses at him so hard he falls over*

| | |
|---|---|
| WEASEL: | *Weasels!* |

*The other WEASELS come*

| | |
|---|---|
| WEASEL: | What you got for me? |
| BLETT: | Found some abandoned burrows in the east meadow, boss. |
| LEAST: | An old human tunnel we can use... |
| WEASEL: | Did you mark them all as weasel? |
| VENKY: | Check. Also found a river-rat and an under-grounder consorting... |
| LEAST: | Yeah, whatever that means, and they're in league with the old black-and-white witchy creature. |
| WEASEL: | The Badger. Interesting. Anything else? |
| VENKY: | *[To LEAST]* You tell him, you're the youngest... |
| BLETT: | *[To VENKY]* You're the oldest... |
| LEAST: | *[To BLETT]* You're the nearest... |
| BLETT: | Well. There was one thing, boss. We did hear this Otter saying he reckoned you didn't, like, really, *know* what the big digging monster was... |
| WEASEL: | You mean Slurpex? |

BLETT:      Yeah Slurpex…

LEAST:      This isn't her saying, right boss, it's this Otter saying, he said, sort of, you didn't really *know* how to control Slurpex, you just –

WEASEL:     I just what.

LEAST:      You've just, sort of, figured out when it goes on and off, like when there's a human sitting in it, or not, sort of thing, so it just *looks* like you control it.

WEASEL:     Really. Interesting. And what do you think of that idea.

LEAST:      I think it's a total lie, boss!

BLETT:      It's a smear, it's a libel!

VENKY:      We told this Otter he better buy a stake in WeaselCo pretty sharpish or get out of the Wood for good, and he said no, so we pushed him in the river.

LEAST:      Splosh!

BLETT:      Few bubbles and he was gone. Ha!

VENKY:      Had to show him who's boss, boss.

WEASEL:     You pushed an Otter in the river. To show him who's boss.

BLETT:      We won't see *him* again, eh!

*WEASEL hisses at them and they recoil*

WEASEL:     *OTTERS LIVE IN THE FLAMING WATER!* (working with amateurs here) *WEASELCO!*

*The FERRETS and STOATS come running*

WEASEL:     Who destroyed your homes?

GANG:       *Slurpex!*

WEASEL:     Who controls Slurpex?

GANG:       *You do!*

WEASEL:     Why do you think I did it?

GANG:    *Um… we're not quite sure but we've got badges and cards and we're happy to let you do all the thinking!*

WEASEL:    Good. And I *am* doing all the thinking. I told Slurpex to – well, *destroy* is such a loaded word, isn't it, I requested that Slurpex *amalgamate* your homes with, well, good old English soil, so that all of us Weasels (including you very educated Ferrets and you very eager, *willing* Stoats) can upgrade to new homes much more befitting our relative status. Do you understand me?

GANG:    *We're not quite sure but we've got badges and –*

WEASEL:    Shut up. It's come to my attention that there are several desirable residences on the far side of the River there, but one property in particular stands virtually empty and unattended. I myself have been inside this house…in a *Dream*…

GANG:    *[In awe]* A *Dream*…

WEASEL:    And in this Dream a Voice said to me: *Weasel, this home is your Destiny*…

GANG:    *Destiny*…

WEASEL:    That's right, this Voice addressed *me*, Weasel, personally. (Later in the Dream it also bought me a beer and gave me its card, but that's my business.)

GANG:    *His business*…

WEASEL:    It is, therefore, my Destiny to live in that beautiful house…

GANG:    *[Ad lib]* His *Destiny*, ahh…

WEASEL:    My old granddad dreamed of living in that house…

GANG:    *[Ad lib]* His old *granddad*, ahh…

| | |
|---|---|
| WEASEL: | Sadly he's now passed away… |
| GANG: | *[Ad lib] Oh no!* ah the poor Weasel I *love* this guy… |
| WEASEL: | So I say to you, if you can't do it for *me* – and who am I? – |
| ERVIN: | Weasel. |
| WEASEL: | (Shut up) If you can't do it for *me* – do it for my poor granddad eh… help my Dream to come true… for your children, and your children's children… |
| GANG: | *[Ad lib]* Children, ahh! Think of the children! Old granddad, ahh! Dream come true, ahhh! *Give us that house NOW!!!* |
| WEASEL: | Let's go, let's go! |

*The WEASEL GANG marches off. The BIRDS set Toad Hall, a big doll's house centre-stage. BADGER, RATTY and MOLE come*

| | |
|---|---|
| RATTY: | There it is, Moley – Toad Hall! |
| MOLE: | I can't quite see, it looks like a little doll's house – |
| RATTY: | It does rather, doesn't it. |
| BADGER: | He used to collect *them*, too. He collected everything. Now he collects empty rooms. |
| RATTY: | He used to collect *friends* and you can see what's left of that. Well, We Happy Few had better start walking. At least we'll have a few moments of peace before – |

*TOAD erupts from somewhere*

| | |
|---|---|
| TOAD: | RATSTER! BADGE! THE QUIET ONE! Our threesome is a foursome! The awesome foursome it *rhymes*! Come on it *must* be true! Let's go, step up, look lively! |
| MOLE: | Awesome foursome hehehe! |
| RATTY: | Aren't you curious why we're here, Toad? |

| | |
|---|---|
| TOAD: | No! Why shouldn't friends want to see The Toad, *I* would! |
| RATTY: | Oh for heaven's sake – |
| BADGER: | Don't you wonder why we look so stern? |
| TOAD: | Ol' Badge, you *always* look stern! *[To MOLE]* Don't listen to 'em, you, what's-your-name, Quiet One – |
| MOLE: | It's Moley – |
| TOAD: | Spoilsports to a man, Molly, don't do *this*, don't do *that*, you stick with me, Mollster! *Ba-naa*! Welcome to Toad Hall! |
| MOLE: | It smells so – |
| TOAD: | Magnificent? Splendid? |
| MOLE: | So – echoey, so empty… |
| TOAD: | That's because it's *ENORMOUS!* |
| MOLE: | Oh! |
| TOAD: | So what do you think, little Moley McMoleface? |
| MOLE: | Er, everything's so, so, so – |
| TOAD: | Fabulous? Incredible? |
| MOLE: | So very – far away… |
| TOAD: | Exactly! What's the point of having money if everything's right beside you? How vulgar would *that* be! If I fancy a bit of nosh I have to walk a good furlong to the Fridge Room, then a short hop to the Buttery and the Serving-Hatch and the Dining Hall, gets me up a grand appetite, y'know, and at every step I can say *it's all the Property of Toad!* Of course I *could* get the servants to help, but, you know… |
| RATTY: | You laid them all off to save money. |
| TOAD: | How vulgar, Ratty, really. The Toad never speaks of money. |

| | |
|---|---|
| MOLE: | Don't you like to – sit by the fire sometimes? |
| TOAD: | Oh, well *that's* a bit of a hike, Molly, through the Gun Room and the Gallery, through the Billiard Room to the Fire Hall, so I prefer to wrap up warm in here and think, you know, warm thoughts. |
| RATTY: | The heating's broken, isn't it, Toad. |

*BADGER finds a big red light-switch*

| | |
|---|---|
| BADGER: | At least the lights still work. Dear me. Get a hold of him, friends! |

*RATTY and MOLE grasp TOAD and sit him down*

| | |
|---|---|
| BADGER: | You knew it would come to this. You've disregarded all my warnings and squandered the money your father left you. And look at you, down to your last chair. |
| TOAD: | It is jolly well *not* my last chair, Badger, there are several chairs left in the Chair Garden, a mere ten-minute walk that way, past the Carpet Hall and the Boot Room and the Napkin House and the Sock Chamber – |
| BADGER: | *ENOUGH!* There is nothing left of your fortune. I shall walk to Town directly, to plead your case at the Bank. In the meantime, the Mole and the Water Rat will keep a close eye on you here, so we know there'll be no more nonsense. |
| RATTY: | It's for your own good, Toady. |
| MOLE: | Badger will take care of everything. |
| BADGER: | So be it. You two: *Do not let him out of your sight. Do not leave the room. Do not listen to his pleas.* He can be an artful, slippery creature. And now for the Town. Maybe I can find out what's gone wrong in the Wild Wood… |

*BADGER sets off grimly*

| | |
|---|---|
| TOAD: | *[To BADGER]* Badge, wait, could you – oh. Too late. |
| RATTY: | Yes, too late, Toad. You've driven us to it. |
| MOLE: | It's not so bad is it, Mr Toad, when friends lend a hand? |
| TOAD: | True, true... uh-uh *[A cough]* very true, good Mollster. I just needed to ask Badger for my – it's nothing. I don't suppose many people will – uh-uh – miss me anyway... |
| MOLE: | Oh, shall I get you some – |
| TOAD: | *[To MOLE]* A toad in my condition, Nurse Molly – uh-uh – *needs* no possessions... that's why I've cast them all to the four winds, you see. I came to this world with nothing, and I – uh-uh – shall leave it the same way... |
| MOLE: | Leave it? I don't understand. Ratty, I think the Toad is in – distress. |
| RATTY: | *[Reading]* Of course he's in distress. Someone stopped the blockhead doing what he pleases for once. |
| MOLE: | He doesn't look quite himself... |
| RATTY: | That'd be a nice change. (7 across:  Six letters beginning and ending with E: 'To get away from somewhere...') |
| MOLE: | He looks a bit peculiar... |
| RATTY: | I know, warts and all, and that big fat mouth of his, but what can you do? Heigh-ho. |

*TOAD mouthes the word 'medication'*

| | |
|---|---|
| MOLE: | 'Madagascar'? Ratty, what's madagascar? |
| RATTY: | It's hot and green and full of splendours, my brother had some high times there... |
| MOLE: | I think he's saying 'medication', Ratty. |

*TOAD faints away with his tongue hanging out*

| | |
|---|---|
| RATTY: | Medication? Good lord, I've never heard of him needing any – no, not even Toad would stoop to that. |
| MOLE: | I don't think he's pretending, Ratty, he was talking about last things, and leaving things, and the four winds oh my! |
| RATTY: | Toad what d'you need, here's a pencil, write it down. |

*TOAD revives enough to scribble something*

| | |
|---|---|
| RATTY: | *Tic-tacs.* Tic-tacs? *The green ones,* righty-ho. Well, better safe than sorry. I'll go, I know the Town a little. You stay here and keep him cheerful, right? |
| MOLE: | I will, don't worry, Ratty! |
| RATTY: | Tic-tacs, the green ones. Dash it, I should be at home, the regatta starts today… |

*RATTY hurries off. TOAD starts whistling 'The Great Escape'*

| | |
|---|---|
| MOLE: | That's a jolly tune, Mr Toad, are you feeling a bit better? |
| TOAD: | Just a… tiny bit, Molly my friend…uh-uh… |
| MOLE: | I'm sure those green tick tocks will set you right. |
| TOAD: | Thank you, Mollsky, thank you, uh-uh, one last request… please lead me to the pearly Gates of Toad Hall, my kind nurse Moll, so I may take my medicine as quickly as possible, for, who knows, uh-uh, I may yet pull through… |
| MOLE: | Aye-aye Mr Toad, help is at hand! |

*MOLE helps TOAD up and they walk towards the Gates*

| | |
|---|---|
| TOAD: | And if it is not to be… think only this of me, uh-uh… |
| MOLE: | Try not to talk, Mr Toad. |

| | |
|---|---|
| TOAD: | That there's some corner of a Cheshire field… |
| MOLE: | And try very hard not to recite poetry. Look here we are at your beautiful gates. Ratty won't be long now. |
| TOAD: | I can hear the world is passing before me… |
| MOLE: | Yes, Ratty says it's the noise from the Town, and the less said the better. |
| TOAD: | It's the open road, can you hear it, Molly? |
| MOLE: | Yes but you're poorly, Mr Toad, d'you not think – |

*TOAD hears cars for the first time*

| | |
|---|---|
| TOAD: | Huh??? That entrancing sound… *neowww… neowww… neowww…* that bewitching smell! *NEOWWW!!!* |

*MOLE runs for cover. A MOTOR CAR comes, driven by WOOLPACK the Judge, with COPPITT the Constable and BOXALL the Gaoler inside*

*TOAD is transfixed by the car. MOLE creeps over to him*

| | |
|---|---|
| MOLE: | Are you feeling better, Toad? |
| TOAD: | Who are you? |
| MOLE: | Oh my, oh dear! |

*The MOTORISTS stuff their faces*

| | |
|---|---|
| WOOLPACK: | 3.5 liter V8 engine. |
| COPPITT: | Plum-colored velour upholstery, like it. |
| BOXALL: | 16 valves, four per cylinder, superb. |
| WOOLPACK: | Alloy wheels as standard. |
| COPPITT: | 300 brake horsepower, like it. |
| WOOLPACK: | Four-pot turbo, excellent. |
| BOXALL: | Superb. |

*They stop, park, and thrust a sign saying THE RED LION into the ground by someone's picnic*

WOOLPACK: Ah, gentlemen, we're in luck, the famous old Red Lion at Grosvenor!

COPPITT: Do they do food? They better do food.

BOXALL: They do do food. Superb.

COPPITT: Like it.

*They help themselves to someone's lunch. TOAD in rapture*

TOAD: A motor car... A *swan*, a *sunbeam,* a *thunderbolt! Poop-poop!* Oh, what could I *be* if I had one of these?

*TOAD lives his dream. MOLE, despite herself, finds it funny*

TOAD: I'd be, I'd be, I'd be the *Toad with a Motor Car,* I'd be the Toad who can't stay long, who has places to be and people to meet, I'd be on the open road, maybe picking up a friend,

*He picks up MOLE*

MOLE: Hehehe!

TOAD: Then dropping her off somewhere because I'm dining with some dignitaries, *dignitaries dignitaries,* then meeting some ordinary people, *Chester 0 Chesterfield 0 was it really? yawn yawn* and then zoom off over here *poop-poop!* and someone might cry out *Slow down, Toad!*

MOLE: Slow down, Toad, hehehe!

TOAD: But the Toad has places to be, and people to meet, and deals and appointments and bargains to make, men to see about dogs, dogs to see about cats, cats to see about fish and fish to be frying, and brains to be picking, and points to be scoring, and *time to be flying!*

*TOAD circles as if he's flying till suddenly he's sitting in the car*

TOAD: Oh I say. Look at me now.

MOLE: Hehehe – huh? Mr Toad you can't *do* that.

TOAD: *Brm...brm...*now, I wonder how it starts...

MOLE:            It's not yours, Mr Toad, it's not right!

*TOAD roars around the space, scattering everything – MOLE runs away.*
*TOAD crashes the car. The MOTORISTS haul him straight into Court.*
*A public gallery assembles*

WOOLPACK:       Court is in session! Lucky for you you'll get a
                fair trial, but *unlucky* for you I'll be presiding
                as I'm the local Magistrate and *that was My*
                *New Motor!*

COPPITT:        Lucky for you we'll hear all the evidence, but
                *unlucky* for you I'll be givin' it as I'm the local
                Constable and you're bang to rights, mate!

BOXALL:         Lucky for you it's a free country, but *unlucky*
                for you it's stuffed full of gaols and I'm the
                local Gaoler and you're comin' with me!

WOOLPACK:       Toad, you've been convicted of the serious
                charge of Spoiling My Afternoon, which
                carries a mandatory sentence, and the
                sentence is:

COURT:          *We don't like your face.*

WOOLPACK:       Therefore you will go to Gaol for ten, any
                advance on ten?

*WOOLPACK takes bids from the audience like an auctioneer*

WOOLPACK:       Twelve…fifteen…twenty…thirty…forty
                years, going, going, GONE!

*WOOLPACK bangs a gavel and the public cheers. TOAD is marched off*
*and thrown in a cell. The BIRDS set the Gaol around him, a wall*
*with twenty chalk marks. RUBY the Gaoler's daughter brings bread*
*and water*

TOAD:           It is the End… The End of Everything…

RUBY:           You only been here twenty minutes, you
                gonna make a right mess of that wall.

TOAD:           That it should come to this, that the Toad,
                the popular and handsome Toad, the – where
                are *you* going?

| | |
|---|---|
| RUBY: | Thought I'd leave you to your moaning. |
| TOAD: | Moaning? Moaning? It's a speech, for crying out loud, it's a *Speech Made by The Toad!* |
| RUBY: | Yeah but it's *about* the Toad so I ain't that bothered. |
| TOAD: | *Ain't that bothered?* It's a major speech, I'm not going to do it in a rotten blummin' cell on my own! |
| RUBY: | Whatever. |
| TOAD: | Now where was I…That it should come – oh the moment's gone. I *was* going to lament for several minutes, we'd both be in tears, and now what? |
| RUBY: | Maybe you should eat. |
| TOAD: | Yes yes, no one's taken my order! Waiter! Garçon! And why have you brought your own dismal little snack in here? |
| RUBY: | This dismal little snack is your dinner, mate. |
| TOAD: | A scrap of bread and a thimble of water, are you out of your mind? I'm the Toad! |
| RUBY: | What and toads don't get hungry. |
| TOAD: | I'm *starving!* I've been rotting in this cell for – |
| RUBY: | Twenty-one minutes. |
| TOAD: | Oh yes, I missed one *[Chalks it on]* I want my supper! |
| RUBY: | Well. You could have a bite of my cheese'n'pickle sandwich, I suppose, but my dad'd be very cross as it's against his regulations. |
| TOAD: | *I want it!* |
| RUBY: | Well… I suppose I could just, maybe, set it down on the ground there, who's gonna notice a single bite… |

*She does and* TOAD *scoffs it*

| | |
|---|---|
| RUBY: | Or something that's freakin' vanished. |
| TOAD: | Now tomorrow I want a roast goose and all the trimmings. |
| RUBY: | Do you Mr Toad. Tomorrow I wanna live in a mansion made of rubies. |
| TOAD: | Oh *I* live in a mansion! It's a self-contained gentleman's residence. Not made of rubies but it may as well be, it's gigantic. You could come and see it. |
| RUBY: | Why. |
| TOAD: | I mean, you could – stand by the main gates or something, you'd see it in the distance, like a little doll's house, ah… You might catch a glimpse of me, racing about, *neeow, neeow,* here there and everywhere. |
| RUBY: | How you gonna do that sat in here then. |
| TOAD: | I…don't know. Hm. So where do *you,* (polite conversation from the Gentlemanly Toad here) where do *you,* um – dwell. |
| RUBY: | Little cottage. |
| TOAD: | Ah, never mind. How many rooms? |
| RUBY: | Hmm, let me count 'em… One. |
| TOAD: | *One???* |
| RUBY: | Eat, sleep, read my book. |
| TOAD: | *One room???* |
| RUBY: | About the size of this cell. |
| TOAD: | Ha ha ha! That's the funniest thing I've *ever heard!* The size of this cell, she goes! Ha ha ha hello I'm in the bedroom, take a step, now I'm in the dining-room, do a twirl, heigh-ho I'm in the ballroom he he he it's a magical house I dwell in! |
| RUBY: | Well *I* like it. |

TOAD:     Do be quiet I'm still laughing…ha ha ha ho ho ho oh oh oh all right I've finished.

RUBY:     I think you're cryin'.

TOAD:     No I'm not.

RUBY:     No I do I think you're cryin'.

TOAD:     Crying with laughter!

RUBY:     Still cryin', though, Mr Toad. Anyway. Strikes me you ain't done such a crime you'd have to rot in here for forty years, so I been thinkin'. I got this aunt, she's a washerwoman…

TOAD:     There there, never mind, I have several aunts who *ought* to be washerwomen.

RUBY:     Oh forget it. You're beyond help you are.

*RUBY leaves*

TOAD:     Ha! Good riddance! Silly girl. Lives in a cottage, ha! Lives in a *[Calls]* You can come back if you like, tell me about your garden that's *this* big, ha! 'Eat, sleep, read me book… me auntie's a washerwoman' silly girl…

*TOAD sighs. Faraway in the Wild Wood, the pan-pipes play*

TOAD:     What the devil is that? Noise-pollution, that is. I'll have those people thrown in – oh. Not much of a sandwich, too much pickle. I'll tell her when I see her, I'll tell whatshername. What *is* her name? All I can see is her silly face, all I can hear is her common little voice 'read me book!' Too much pickle. Not confused… a bit confused… confused.

*He sighs. BOXALL comes*

BOXALL:   Get up, you. Ten seconds exercise.

TOAD:     Ten seconds, *ten seconds*, that's not fair! I
          haven't exercised in ten *years*, I won't last *one*
          second!

*BOXALL marches TOAD away*

*BADGER, RATTY and MOLE hurry towards Toad Hall squabbling*

BADGER:   Green tictacs, Rat, how *could* you, you river-
          dwelling *halfwit*, how could you fall for that?

RATTY:    Better safe than sorry, old girl, I didn't know
          this little nubbins was going to lead him right
          to the gates!

MOLE:     I'm *not* a nubbins, I don't know what he's
          like, if it weren't for you I'd be safe and snug
          in my own cosy parlour!

BADGER:   Forty years my foot, no one was hurt, for
          heaven's sake.

MOLE:     I'm not a nubbins, Ratty.

RATTY:    I accept you're not a nubbins, it's just that –

*THREE WEASELS block their way*

LEAST:    Where d'you think *you're* going.

RATTY:    Toad Hall, if it's any of your beeswax.

BLETT:    Stop right there, I would.

VENKY:    Ain't no Toad Hall, you must be lost.

BADGER:   That large white building yonder, dimwit, it
          belongs to a friend of ours, and –

LEAST:    I don't think so.

BLETT:    What's Toad Hall?

LEAST:    Search me. Anyone know?

VENKY:    You mean *that* building? Sign doesn't say
          Toad Hall.

LEAST:    Sign says WEASEL TOWERS.

RATTY:    Good lord, you can't do that, it's private
          property, it's –

*The WEASEL GANG come with sticks and clubs. WEASEL comes too*

WEASEL: Oh look, if it isn't All Creatures Great and Small… *[To BADGER] You*, go home to your hole in the ground, *[To RATTY] you*, be off to your weedy old pond, *[To MOLE]* and *you*, just crawl back to wherever it is you come from.

MOLE: Oh, well, if you wouldn't mind showing me where that is, perhaps I can –

*WEASEL hisses at MOLE, who falls over. RATTY and BADGER shield her. The GANG hiss, raise their sticks and the FRIENDS flee. The GANG whoop, form a line, start bowing and chatting ad lib because they think the play is over and they're actors again. WEASEL watches them, aghast*

WEASEL: *What the hell do you think you're doing?*

POOL: Curtain-call, it's over, we won!

WEASEL: *Get back in here!* It's not over! It ain't over till I say it's over! Now, I know that in many ways it's been a team effort, but above all we owe our victory to one special individual: me. Credit where credit's due, and, as you all know, you owe me *a lot of credit*. Tonight we will celebrate The Personal Triumph of Lord Weasel of Weasel Towers with a Victory Banquet! You all have jobs to do!

GANG: Yes boss!

WEASEL: *[To LEAST]* You, prepare to stuff your face.

LEAST: Will do!

WEASEL: *[To BLETT]* You, prepare to get royally drunk.

BLETT: Wahay!

WEASEL: *[To VENKY]* You, prepare to stuff your face, get royally drunk, and make a total git of yourself on the dance-floor.

VENKY: Copy that, boss!

*The WEASELS run off*

WEASEL: *[To SIP]* You, prepare the hors d'oeuvres.

SIP: Oh. (Well I'll do gazpacho and those little vol-au-vents…)

WEASEL: *[To POOL]* You, two main courses.

POOL: Right. (Maybe steak au poivre plus a vegetable option?)

WEASEL: *[To FINICAL]* You. Run around swearing at them very loudly.

FINICAL: You got it. (Where the *[BEEEEEEEP]* is my ratatouille?)

*The FERRETS run off*

ERVIN: Er. What about us stoats, mister.

JILL: Salt-of-the-earth, us, remember.

WEASEL: You? Go and stand all night in the cold, guarding the gates. North Gate, East Gate, Fore Gate. You're Stoat Troop.

STOATS: Yay. Stoat Troop. Woohoo.

*Off they go, leaving WEASEL all alone. He looks at us*

WEASEL: And as for you lot: twenty minutes. Eat. Drink. Get on my good side.

*He hisses at us all*

WEASEL: Simples.

*END OF ACT ONE*

# ACT TWO

*TOAD in Gaol. A few more chalk marks and a rubbish sketch of Ruby. Ruby's AUNT DORIS is sorting the laundry*

DORIS:  O! Woe! The injustice! That it should come to this! Dirty sheets in a filthy ol' gaol. I 'ad hopes, I 'ad dreams I did, I was the finest washerwoman of my day I was, I coulda cleaned for the county, I coulda laundered for England, my greatness has been wasted on a world that just don't care.

TOAD:  Really? Me too, old stout lady, *my* greatness has also been –

DORIS:  I coulda lathered for lords and ladies, I coulda rinsed for royalty, I coulda soaped for the stars! But no, I been forgotten.

TOAD:  Hm, me too, honest plump woman, I too have been forgotten! I've been here three whole hours, and no one's come to –

DORIS:  I was the finest scrubber of my day!

TOAD:  Look shut up, big poor person, *I'm* talking –

*RUBY comes*

RUBY:  You are a whiny, selfish, moaning, charmless blob of self-pity.

TOAD:  *[To DORIS]* You *are*, you know, I was just going to say that –

RUBY:  Not her, *you.* So I want you out of here. I don't care what the sentence is. Or if my dad loses his job over it, it's a rotten job and it's making *him* rotten. Take your clothes off.

TOAD:  Eh? Good lord, what *is* this place?

RUBY:  Just do it. You too, Auntie Doris. You two have exactly the same figure.

| | |
|---|---|
| TOAD: | She's not slim! |
| DORIS: | I ain't a fatso! |
| TOAD: | *What?* |
| RUBY: | *Do it!* Shut up and swap your uniforms. You get your freedom, you get your chocolate orange. |
| DORIS: | Ooh, lovely. |
| TOAD: | Good grief, I don't look anything like her! |
| RUBY: | You'll look like a washerwoman, that's all that matters. My dad won't notice, he don't notice anything, he ain't noticed me for years. |
| TOAD: | Really? I noticed you – I mean – I noticed you were around. I mean you never stop talking. |
| RUBY: | Such a charmer you are. There, that should do it. |

*Now TOAD is a washerwoman and DORIS a prisoner*

| | |
|---|---|
| TOAD: | I look ridiculous! |
| RUBY: | Perfect. Now it should look like you overpowered her, Toad. |
| TOAD: | Well I'm not going to bash her in, you silly girl. |
| RUBY: | You don't have to, fool, just tie her up. |
| DORIS: | Yes, yes, tie me up! |
| TOAD: | We don't have any rope, you daft woman. |
| DORIS: | You can use your tie. |
| TOAD: | Oh yes, well, all right… |
| DORIS: | Or your braces. |
| TOAD: | Oh lordy, in for a penny… |
| DORIS: | Or your belt or your shoelace. Or these ribbons I happen to have on my person. |

*DORIS produces ribbons with which RUBY and TOAD tie her up*

| | |
|---|---|
| DORIS: | But there ain't no call to gag me. |
| TOAD/RUBY: | *[Gagging her.]* Yes there is. |
| RUBY: | Now go out the way you came. |
| TOAD: | Aren't you coming? |
| RUBY: | Why would I. |
| TOAD: | I – don't know, it would be, well – company. |
| RUBY: | I'll watch you to the canal. Follow the towpath west about eight miles and you'll know where you are again. Or hitch a ride on one of the barges. But don't drop out of character, Toad, they all know your face round here. |
| TOAD: | Oh they do, do they… |
| RUBY: | Not in a good way. Off you go then. Have a nice life in your mansion. Go on, scoot! |

*TOAD looks at her, and hurries away*

| | |
|---|---|
| RUBY: | Yeah. Don't mention it. – Come with me, Auntie, I'm gonna put you in the cupboard. Wanted to for years, I can tell you. |

*RUBY goes, taking the trussed-up DORIS. BOXALL comes with a great chain of keys, and TOAD from another way, as washerwoman*

| | |
|---|---|
| BOXALL: | Who goes there? |
| TOAD: | Woe, woe, I 'ad hopes, I 'ad dreams… That it should come to this, etcetera! |
| BOXALL: | Oh it's you, sis. You sound like that stupid fat Toad. |
| TOAD: | No I don't, I sound like the stupid fat washerwoman – I mean I *am* the stupid fat washerwoman, and that's why I sound like her – I mean like me. |
| BOXALL: | Thinkin' about it, sis, you also *look* a bit like that stupid fat Toad. |

| TOAD: | I most certainly do not, and stop calling him fat, what he is is big-boned. |
| BOXALL: | You're right, sis, that Toad is a big fat big-boned fatso and no mistake. What's the matter with you? |
| TOAD: | *[Clenched] Nothing. I agree with you.* |
| BOXALL: | You agree that that Toad is a big fat fatso? |
| TOAD: | *[Very clenched] Yes. I…agree that Toad is a big fat fatso.* |
| BOXALL: | Big brother knows best eh, sis, off you trot now. |

*TOAD goes past BOXALL and does a little triumphant leap in the air – he's free! From another direction, DORIS struggles in her bonds*

| DORIS: | Help! Help me! Please, I've been mercilessly bound in – oh. Call that a *knot?* Amateurs. |

*She gets free and goes. The BIRDS set up the canal. BESS the Bargewoman moors her barge, humming to herself. She gapes in wonder seeing TOAD as a washerwoman*

| TOAD: | *[To himself]* A barge, a barge! – Ahoy there, rustic humming person, may I hitch a ride on your quaint retro-style river-craft? … Er – did I say something strange? I am simply a stupid big-boned washerwoman in need of conveyance towards Toad Hall, where I shall at last reveal my true nature. |
| BESS: | I do – not – believe it. |
| TOAD: | Why not, the Gaoler did. |
| BESS: | Oh my Gawd it's *you*! |
| TOAD: | Yes it is – no it's not – no it is – yes it's not – what on earth do you mean? |
| BESS: | It's you, the one they speak of in hushed tones! |
| TOAD: | Well yes, that's true, keep going… |

| | |
|---|---|
| BESS: | You're the lost genius of washing, you're the great wasted talent who could have laundered for England, rinsed for royalty, and soaped for the stars! |
| TOAD: | You were doing fine up to 'lost genius'. |
| BESS: | What a day to meet *you* of all people! It's like a miracle! Of *course* you can have a ride on my barge, it would be the most incredible honour of my whole life! Climb aboard! |

*TOAD climbs aboard*

| | |
|---|---|
| TOAD: | Where's first-class, I don't half fancy a bucks fizz… |
| BESS: | No one told us you were coming! |
| TOAD: | Well I like a surprise. |
| BESS: | Everybody's waiting! |
| TOAD: | What. |
| BESS: | Contestants, contestants, our Guest Judge is here! |

*Suddenly EIGHT WASHERWOMEN appear from nowhere*

| | |
|---|---|
| BESS: | Welcome one and all, to the Great English Wash-Off, where eight amateur washerwomen will compete for the crown of England's Finest Amateur Launderer, and here to judge you all is – well it's a dream come true for me – it's the legendary Lost Genius of Laundry, Doris Boxall! |

*The WASHERWOMEN idolize TOAD*

| | |
|---|---|
| TOAD: | Oh, yes, right, well, jolly good, Lost Genius it is… |
| BESS: | Now, Mrs Jakes, what are you washing for us today? |
| MRS JAKES: | Well, Bess, I'm going to be washing this white texture modern luxury slim-fit shirt on |

|  | a Delicate cycle using a non-chlorine-based detergent. |
|---|---|
| BESS: | Marvellous. What do you think, Doris? |
| TOAD: | I – yes, do that. Wash things. |
| BESS: | Hahaha that's what it's all about eh! Mrs Povey, what've you got for us there? |
| MRS POVEY: | I'm going to be cleaning this silk scarf, Bess, using a mild, non-alkaline baby shampoo in a lukewarm handwash introducing distilled vinegar at the rinse stage. |
| BESS: | Crikey that's ambitious! Doris Boxall? |
| TOAD: | Um… get things clean. |
| BESS: | Er, right. Well good luck to you all. But first, on this extra special occasion, with the legendary Doris Boxall here among us mortals, I'm sure our contestants have some questions they're dying to ask you! Over to you, contestants! |

*TOAD is mobbed by the WASHERWOMEN asking technical laundry questions ad lib, until he breaks free, and rips his costume off*

| TOAD: | I don't know! I don't care! Do your own ruddy washing! Pay someone to do it! *I am not a Washerwoman!* I do *not* lather for lords and ladies, and I most certainly do *not* soap for the stars! I would have you know that I am The Toad! The popular, handsome, ingenious and charming Toad of Toad Hall! I do not *do* things for people, people *do* things for *me!* Now, humble boat-person and your laundering posse, I demand you start up the engines and ferry me in style to the banks of my Ancestral Seat! |
|---|---|
| BESS: | Ladies, *I* say – let's do the dirty washing! |

*BESS and the WASHERWOMEN chase TOAD around the space until they catch him and put him through the wash-cycle they're describing*

WASHERWOMEN: *Soak a swab in alcohol*
*Scrub the oily stains away*
*Fill a tub with baby wash*
*Mix the suds and shake the spray*
*Dab it on a fibre cloth*
*Wipe until you see your face*
*Hang it somewhere hot and wet*
*Keep it in a cool dry place*

*BESS and the WASHERWOMEN throw TOAD in the canal, and the barge chugs away. He emerges in a long white shirt. RUBY's there*

RUBY: That went well.

TOAD: Look at me! I'm soaking wet, my white shirt's ruined, and it's undone to the waist, I look terrible!

RUBY: Wouldn't say that.

TOAD: What?

RUBY: Nothing.

TOAD: Why are you here, anyway? Come to laugh at me, I suppose.

RUBY: Well yeah, mainly that, but now I'm done laughing, here's some cocoa and a pie.

TOAD: *[Taking it]* Ooh, pie.

RUBY: Couldn't stretch to roast goose and the trimmings.

TOAD: *[Eating]* No? S'pose not at short notice. Oh well. Not sated... almost sated... sated. Thank you.

RUBY: *Thank you???* – huh! – did he just say the words –

RATTY: Toady! There he is!

*RATTY, MOLE and BADGER greet TOAD*

MOLE: Mr Toad, Mr Toad!

| TOAD: | Mollster! Rattington! Badge! |
| RATTY: | We heard you'd been sprung somehow. |
| TOAD: | Sprung *m'self*, old boy! Great escape and all that. |
| BADGER: | Some while since I've been this happy to see *you*. |
| MOLE: | The awesome foursome hehehe! |
| BADGER: | We got your sentence reduced on appeal, from forty years to two hours. They do say the Law is an ass. Lucky for you the appeal judge was a donkey. |
| TOAD: | Oh it was terrible in there. I was in chains, y'know. |
| RUBY: | No you weren't. He wasn't. |
| TOAD | *[To RUBY]* You can go now, by the way. |
| RATTY: | Made a friend there, Toady? |
| MOLE: | Hullo… |
| TOAD: | Oh no, no, that's just a, you know, a *girl*, *eeuuww*… |
| RUBY: | Goodbye, Toad. |
| RATTY: | Come along, old chap, we've got a lot of news to tell you, and none of it's very good… |

*RUBY walking away, TOAD watching her go*

| MOLE: | Who is she, Mr Toad, would she like to come with us? |
| TOAD: | Oh no, no. Not a bad sort, but she – she finds me ridiculous. |

*MOLE pats him on the back, and they walk on*

*MONTAGE: the STOATS come through, armed with sticks*

| HOB: | All I'm sayin' is, how can you tell we're Guards if we don't have badges that *say* we're Guards? |

| | |
|---|---|
| JILL: | Well I know you're a prat but you don't have a badge that *says* 'I'm a prat'. |
| HOB: | Ha! You just said 'I'm a prat'. |
| JILL: | Ha! *You* just said 'I'm a prat' and no returns. |
| ERVIN: | Hey we won't be Guards for long, guys, cos soon them snobby ferrets'll take a turn bein' Guards, and then them bossy weasels'll take a turn bein' cooks, and we'll get to be the guests at the Great Feast, cos it'll all go round in rotation sort of. |
| JILL: | Eh? What the hell makes you think it'll 'all go round in rotation sort of'? |
| ERVIN: | Well, it's like, y'know…fair. |

*HOB and JILL look at ERVIN, and each other*

| | |
|---|---|
| HOB/JILL: | Prat. |

*The FERRETS come with Waitrose shopping*

| | |
|---|---|
| POOL: | Did you clock that stoat in the frozen foods? Can they not shop at Lidl like all the other stoats? |
| SIP: | Toad's old kitchen, chaps, it's really something. Cool clean lines but offset with a rustic simplicity. |
| FINICAL: | *You:* slice the parsnips. *You:* fry the onions. *You:* have a meltdown and start crying in the larder. *You:* say you quit and call me a *[BEEEEEP]*. Let's cook! |

*The WEASELS in black tie, already plastered*

| | |
|---|---|
| VENKY: | Oggy oggy oggy! |
| LEAST/BLETT: | Oi oi oi! |
| LEAST: | Hey what d'you call a mole on a lawnmower – |
| BLETT: | No I got one, what d'you get when you cross a rat and a ferret – |

| | |
|---|---|
| VENKY: | Shut up, so a vole, a bat and a badger go into a pub, right – |

*WEASEL, dressed to the nines*

| | |
|---|---|
| VENKY: | Oggy oggy oggy! |
| LEAST/BLETT: | Oi oi oi! |

*RATTY, MOLE and TOAD in a cacophony, BADGER shaking her head*

| | |
|---|---|
| RATTY: | /I tell you there's hundreds of 'em, weasels, ferrets, stoats and what-have-you, armed to the teeth and in no mood to compromise, I say we mobilize all of our friends on the river-bank!/ |
| MOLE: | /Maybe if we all sat down and tried to understand each other, I mean, I don't understand anything but if we sat down over tea and biscuits, or fondant fancies, don't you think we might all start to get along?/ |
| TOAD: | /I'll have 'em thrown in Gaol, I will – no Gaol's too good for 'em – I'll have 'em thrown in the river – not dirty enough for 'em – I'll have 'em thrown in a filthy great 'orrible puddle you see if I don't!/ |
| BADGER: | *All of you be QUIET!* – My friends. This is a dark situation and it's going to take some bright minds to put it right. |
| RATTY: | That's what we're doing here, old girl, it's just they won't listen to me – |
| TOAD: | I'm the brightest mind around for miles, Badge, I single-handedly escaped from Gaol in disguise – |
| BADGER: | *Be quiet!* Now. Mole… |
| RATTY: | Oh yes, ask Moley, do, she'll invite them all over for tea and crumpets on the river-bank – |
| BADGER: | Mr Water Rat! Enough. Now, Mole: when I was a young badger in the prime of youth, |

|  | I had the ability to sense the presence of young creatures. Then I grew older and that gift eroded, but I believe, little snuffler, that you still possess it. |
|---|---|

TOAD: Come off it, Badge, poor old Mollster here can't see a blummin' thing, I mean, it's part of her charm and all, but –

BADGER: Shut up, Toad, you whiny, selfish, moaning –

TOAD: 'Charmless blob of self-pity' I know, I've been told.

BADGER: I'm not talking about *seeing*, I am talking about *knowing*. Well, Mole?

MOLE: Oh, oh my, perhaps, sometimes I – I sense they're close, I do.

BADGER: I want you to take Mr Rat, Mr Toad and myself along the river-bank, and I want you to show us where the young creatures are. We shall ask them politely to tell us *everything* they know about the weasels, ferrets and stoats who have invaded Toad Hall. I want to know what they like. I want to know what they *don't* like. And I want to know what they're doing right now. When we know all these things, we shall make our plans accordingly. Let's go. *Go!*

*MOLE seeks young creatures who might be helpful. RATTY and BADGER jot their information down in notebooks while TOAD helps himself to people's picnics. BADGER leads them off to prepare their assault on Toad Hall. Meanwhile the STOATS are on guard, shivering*

ERVIN: Ha. Showed 'em.

HOB: Showed 'em what.

ERVIN: Showed 'em who's boss.

JILL: *How* do you reckon we showed 'em who's boss.

| | |
|---|---|
| ERVIN: | Them all stuck inside the house, ha! while we get to be the heroes out here! Result! |
| JILL: | *[To HOB]* Do *you* wanna beat him up, or shall I. |
| HOB: | *[To JILL]* Knock yourself out. |

*BADGER comes, in a hat*

| | |
|---|---|
| HOB: | Who goes there? |
| BADGER: | Badge delivery for Stoat Troop. |
| ERVIN: | Badges, *yesss!* |
| JILL: | *We're* Stoat Troop, we ain't expectin' no badge delivery. |
| BADGER: | I'm sorry, I thought you were Guards. |
| STOATS: | We are, we're Guards, we're Stoat Troop! |
| BADGER: | And so I've made you your badges. I am, after all, a badger. |

*BADGER shows them three GUARD badges, a big red one, a small red one, and a blue one*

| | |
|---|---|
| JILL: | Hang on, we're on the *lookout* for a badger… |
| HOB: | Yeah but this one's got a hat, she's official. |
| ERVIN: | And we need badges, *yay!* |

*BADGER gives out the badges*

| | |
|---|---|
| STOATS: | Stoat Troop! |
| HOB: | Hang on, yours is bigger. |
| JILL: | Mine's the wrong colour. |
| ERVIN: | No, *mine's* the wrong colour! |
| STOATS: | Swapsies yay! |

*They swap the badges*

| | |
|---|---|
| STOATS: | Stoat Troop! |

*They realise they have the wrong ones again*

| | |
|---|---|
| JILL: | Hang on, yours is bigger. |
| HOB: | Mine's the wrong colour. |

ERVIN:        No, *mine's* the wrong colour!

STOATS:      Swapsies yay!

*They swap the badges*

STOATS:      Stoat Troop!

*They realise they have the wrong ones again. By now BADGER, RATTY, TOAD and MOLE are long gone. The STOATS run off arguing in three different wrong directions*

*The Kitchens: the FERRETS frantically preparing food. RATTY, BADGER, MOLE and TOAD come with clipboards*

POOL:         Hey get out, we're cooking here!

SIP:            I need those aubergines *now*!

FINICAL:     Wait a sec, they've got clipboards…

RATTY:        In the name of Her Majesty's Government, this is a snap inspection by the standards agency OFFSNOB. We have reason to believe that these kitchens are infested with *mustela putorius*, which is in contravention notwithstanding howsoever therewithal etcetera etcetera.

*RATTY and the FRIENDS hand them documents*

POOL:         Hm, good use of 'notwithstanding…'

SIP:            *Triplicate!* White, yellow, pink for my own records – *yesss!*

FINICAL:     *[Reading]* Ah look it has a *sub-section 19b*, they mean business, team.

POOL/SIP:    Business!

RATTY:        You'll be able to plead your case to the Contravention Committee currently Convening in the Convention Centre, all the way down that corridor. You also have the legal right to know who reported these infractions.

POOL:         Yeah, who snitched on us?

| | |
|---|---|
| RATTY: | Oh, *mustela erminea.* |
| POOL: | Stoats! |
| SIP: | What a surprise! |
| FINICAL: | Come on, team, tool up and let's *do it* – let's file counterclaims! |

*The FERRETS collect documents and go, as the FRIENDS slip past*

| | |
|---|---|
| TOAD: | HOME AGAIN! |
| BADGER/RATTY/<br>MOLE: | *Ssshhh!!!* |
| MOLE: | Hehehe, 'badges', that was so clever, Mrs B! |
| BADGER: | And bravo, Rat, you knew how to fool those ferrets. |
| RATTY: | So, Toad, you said you had a *plan to defeat the weasels.* What is it? Time to share. |
| TOAD: | Oh yes, well it's devilishly simple, chaps. It's GENIUS! |
| BADGER/RATTY/<br>MOLE: | *Ssshhh!!!* |
| TOAD: | Well, we wait outside the Banqueting Hall… |
| BADGER: | Ye-es… |
| RATTY: | There's about forty of 'em now, remember. |
| TOAD: | Big deal, and we… |
| MOLE: | We, what, it's so exciting hehehe! |
| TOAD: | It is, isn't it? we… creep up to the door, then we open the door softly, then we… |
| BADGER: | What? |
| RATTY: | We what? |
| TOAD: | WE… WHACK 'EM AND WHOP 'EM AND BASH 'EM AND BEAT 'EM AND POUND 'EM AND PUNCH 'EM AND KNOCK 'EM AND NUT 'EM AND – |

| | |
|---|---|
| BADGER/RATTY/<br>MOLE: | *Ssshhh!!!* |
| RATTY: | *That's* your plan to defeat the weasels? |
| BADGER: | We're outnumbered, you fool, you puffed-up pond-dwelling fatuous *bobblehead!* |
| TOAD: | I'm not fatuous, I'm big-boned! |
| MOLE: | You're a nubbins, Toad, I'm sorry but you're a nubbins! |

*Angry WEASELS, FERRETS and STOATS audible at every point*

| | |
|---|---|
| BADGER: | And you've given the game away. Stoats, with sticks. |
| RATTY: | They've rumbled us – ferrets! With assorted stationery. |
| MOLE: | That way too, oh my, weasels, so many weasels! |
| BADGER: | Well. My friends. We must put up a brave fight. |
| RATTY: | I dreamed one day I'd make a heroic stand. Except – in the dream I've got a cricket bat… |
| BADGER: | Perhaps the Great Piper-in-the-Trees will help us now. |
| RATTY: | Get 'em in singles, Ratty, get 'em in singles… |
| TOAD: | Save me, someone, I'm the Toad, I'm the Toad! |
| MOLE: | WILL YOU SHUT UP! |

*Astonishment*

| | |
|---|---|
| MOLE: | *[To TOAD] Just stop your pathetic whimpering!* |
| RATTY: | She's right, Toad, stiff upper lip now. |
| MOLE: | *[To RATTY] And YOU! Just stop it with your stiff lips and your sticky wickets and your never-ending picnics!* |

BADGER:     It *does* get quite annoying, Rat, your idiom –

MOLE:       *[To BADGER] And YOU! Stop saying deep wise weird words I don't quite understand!* Toad, where are the lights?

TOAD:       What? The switch over there. You can't switch the lights off, you nubbins – I DON'T LIKE THE DARK!

MOLE:       Oh but *I* do.

*MOLE switches the big switch, removes her glasses, sniffs the air*

MOLE:       I know where they all are. Do what I say. Get ready.

*The WEASELS, FERRETS and STOATS run in, suddenly blind. MOLE guides the FRIENDS to victory, à la Crouching Mole, Hidden Dragon*

MOLE:       Ratty, right behind you – Toad, six o'clock – Badger, north-north-east – Ratty, hard a'starboard – Toad, make mine a double – Badger, twenty-past-seven – Ratty, left arm spinner – Badger, whisky-and-ginger – Moley, time for a *BISCUIT!*

*MOLE knocks WEASEL for six. BADGER switches the light back on. The FRIENDS stand tall among the groggy, beaten remnants of the WEASEL GANG. The last ones standing are simply pushed over by TOAD and crawl away. Celebration!*

TOAD:       Take that, ha! By a knockout in the fifth!

BADGER:     My friends, ours is the Victory!

RATTY:      Bowled 'em out! Hole-in-one! They think it's all over…

TOAD/BADGER/
RATTY:      *IT IS NOW!*

MOLE:       We were the awesome/four –

BADGER:     /I believe the Piper heard our prayers!

RATTY:      In the final over! By a whisker in the home straight!

| | |
|---|---|
| TOAD: | Whacked 'em and whopped 'em and stomped 'em and stuffed 'em! |
| MOLE: | We were the/awesome – |
| TOAD: | /Last time they'll pick a fight with the Toad! |
| BADGER: | I *knew* those poor little stoats would fall for the badges, |
| RATTY: | And *I* knew the ferrets were itching for a fight, eh, that was me, and I think we're forgetting someone… |
| MOLE: | Oh, it was nothing much – |
| RATTY: | Our agents in the field! *[The audience]* |
| BADGER: | We couldn't have done it without our brilliant spies! |

*BADGER, RATTY and TOAD applaud the audience. MOLE forgotten*

| | |
|---|---|
| TOAD: | Home is what matters! |
| MOLE: | Hear hear, and when I've found my/way home, I'd – |
| TOAD: | /Whether we live in grand palatial splendour like for example myself, or dismal catacombs like you, Badge, or a tiny cottage with one room to eat and sleep and read your book in, Home is where the heart is! |
| BADGER/RATTY: | Hear hear! |
| MOLE: | Hear hear, which is why I'd like to invite/ you all to – |
| TOAD: | /I hereby declare that I shall restore Toad Hall to its ancient magnificence! |
| RATTY: | Well I'm off home to watch what's left of the regatta… |
| BADGER: | I must find out what's gone wrong with all these stoats and ferrets and weasels… |
| TOAD: | Here's to a famous victory – the Battle of Toad Hall! |

BADGER/RATTY:    Hear hear!

*MOLE has slipped away. The* BIRDS *try to tell them about her*

TOAD:    Hey even the *Birds* are singing about the Toad!

RATTY:    That's quite a racket. Maybe something's up…

BADGER:    Listen… *Mole*. Mole? Snuffler?

RATTY:    Moley?

TOAD:    Where the devil are you, Mollster?

RATTY:    She was right there!

BADGER:    She's not now. We were all so wrapped up in our victory, we forgot who the real hero was.

RATTY:    She played a damn fine innings.

TOAD:    I suppose she *did* make a contribution.

RATTY:    Dammit Toady, she saved our bacon and we've jolly well let her down.

BADGER:    She must have gone to look for her home.

RATTY:    Which means she's in the Wild Wood.

BADGER:    Alone. With all those who mean us harm.

RATTY:    Oh lord, oh no…

BADGER:    Right, there are three paths through the Wood from here, we'll have to split up. Who'll take the Path of Danger?

TOAD:    Danger *eeuuww*. I think I'll pass on that one, Badge.

RATTY:    This is my fault. I'll find her. Or I shan't come back at all.

*RATTY runs off.* BADGER *looks down another path*

BADGER:    That way's the Path of Darkness.

| | |
|---|---|
| TOAD: | Ah, yes, well the thing with *darkness* is, the old condition, you know – uh-uh – you see no one got me my tic-tacs… |
| BADGER: | I'll take it, I know it well. Good luck, Toad, you go that way. |
| TOAD: | Er, yes, righty-ho, this way being, the – ? |
| BADGER: | Path of Death. |

*BADGER runs off down the Path of Darkness*

| | |
|---|---|
| TOAD: | Right. Path of – hmm. It's probably named after a man called *De'Ath.* Colonel De'Ath. Path of De'Ath, yes that's it. Well, no one's looking, I *could* just toddle off to bed… wouldn't be much use, would I, I was pretty hopeless back there, I suppose. Only… poor Mollster, all alone. I see I shall have to be brave. I know, I'll make a song of how brave I'm being. Ahem. *When the Toad saved the day,/the Birds were all a-twitter, and the…*what rhymes with *twitter*, hmm… |

*TOAD tiptoes down the Path of Death*

*WEASEL and the battered WEASELS*

| | |
|---|---|
| LEAST: | It's true, boss, the rumour's true! |
| BLETT: | That little four-eyes is alone in the wood! |
| VENKY: | Got no clue where it's going! |
| WEASEL: | You two follow it. You, come with me. There's a place beyond the wood, my spies think they've found the molehill. Slurpex is up there in the meadow, awaiting my orders. |
| LEAST: | Are we gonna move in, boss? |
| BLETT: | Let's take it for the weasels! Revenge! |
| WEASEL: | No one is taking it. No one's going to live there. Because we're going to fill it up with *mud.* You know, fellers, sometimes being a weasel means showing your true colours. |

>When the little four-eyes sees what we've
done to her place, she'll wish she was deaf
and dumb as well as blind.

*WEASEL and VENKY go one way, LEAST and BLETT another*

*RATTY alone*

RATTY:          Moley, it's me Ratty, we're going to find
                your home! Moley, please, I know a fine spot
                for a midnight feast!

*RATTY hears the pan-pipes*

RATTY:          *Take the adventure, heed the call...* I dreamed of
                this hour, but I'm not dreaming now... Time
                to step up for once, time to play that innings.
                Moley!

*RATTY hurries on, BADGER comes, hears a second pan-pipe*

BADGER:         Help us now, Great Piper, in our time of
                trial, help us find our friend. And if you do
                need a new companion, take a wise old fool
                like me.

*BADGER hurries on. The pan-pipes fade. TOAD comes*

TOAD:           *Wh-wh-when the T-t-t-toad s-s-saved the d-d-
                day – the b-b-birds were all a t-t-twitter, pint
                of bitter, spam fritter,* nothing fits, the world's
                forgotten how to rhyme!

RUBY:           How about *He needed a babysitter.*

*RUBY with her rucksack. TOAD jumps a mile*

TOAD:           Help I'm being waylaid! – oh.

RUBY:           I'm trying to see the world and you keep
                getting in the way.

TOAD:           Oh, you, you must be terrified, a *girl* all
                alone in the woods!

RUBY:           Petrified. Yikes. Brr.

TOAD:           You could do with, y'know, a companion,
                chap with a bit of backbone.

RUBY:       Yeah but you'll do till I find one.

TOAD:       Look I am a Vertebrate, you know.

RUBY:       Well that's lucky, what with me being
            terrified and so on. Better hold my hand, eh.

TOAD:       Er, well, yes, if it'd make you feel better.

RUBY:       It would. My name's Ruby Boxall.

TOAD:       Pleased to meet you, my name is –

*She takes TOAD's hand and their eyes meet*

TOAD:       I have no idea…

*The pan-pipes come again. They go. Now MOLE, very scared*

MOLE:       Oh my, oh my… I know it's a shabby, dingy
            little place, not like Ratty's, or Badger's, or
            Toad Hall, but it was my own little home
            and I was fond of it, and I *want* it, oh my…
            and what's the point of having friends, they
            probably haven't even noticed I'm missing!
            Oh my little parlour, the comfy chair was
            *there*, the fireplace was *there*… and the
            lamp…

*She hears the pan-pipes*

MOLE:       The god-of-little-creatures! *His* heart's
            beating too! Oh little creature, show me the
            way home, like you used to long ago…

*MOLE stumbles off. LEAST and BLETT, looking uneasily two ways*

LEAST:      I hate that noise, that's the Devil-in-the-
            woods that is.

BLETT:      Look at Slurpex there, it's like he's *watching*
            us.

LEAST:      Shut up, will you, the boss controls him!

BLETT:      Does he? does he? what if he only *thinks* he
            does?

*LEAST and BLETT go off after MOLE*

*TOAD & RUBY come, hand-in-hand. RUBY stops, looks off*

| | |
|---|---|
| RUBY: | Wait, Mr Toad – what's that over there in the meadow? |
| TOAD: | Some big yellow machine, I'm not getting in that, I got forty years for that – |
| RUBY: | You got three hours. It's a digger – looks like it's been abandoned. |
| TOAD: | We have to find the Mollster! |
| RUBY: | Yes but if she saw *that* she'll have gone the other way – |
| TOAD: | What? Yes you're right! You're a girl and you're right! |
| RUBY: | Whole new world, eh Mr Toad? |
| TOAD: | Not new – almost new – completely new! |

*They run off together*

*MOLE finds her home. WEASEL and VENKY found it already*

| | |
|---|---|
| MOLE: | Oh my! I'm ho – ho – oh. |
| WEASEL: | You've got visitors. |
| MOLE: | I – haven't – any biscuits – |
| WEASEL: | You don't need any biscuits. You don't need anything at all, four-eyes, because we ripped your door off its hinges. |
| MOLE: | Oh, oh my – |
| WEASEL: | Then we threw all your things on the floor. |
| MOLE: | No – |
| WEASEL: | And then we filled your house with mud. |
| MOLE: | No, not my – my – |
| VENKY: | Boss let's leave it, this don't feel right! |

*VENKY runs away*

| | |
|---|---|
| WEASEL: | You don't have any friends in the world. You don't even have a home. |

*The pipes grow louder and* MOLE *faints at her door. The pipes stop*

RATTY, BADGER *and* TOAD *with* RUBY *run in from different directions. They go to the fallen* MOLE, *try to revive her*

RATTY:              Moley? Moley old chap?

RUBY:               Poor dab.

BADGER:             Her heart's beating.

TOAD:               There we go.

BADGER:             But I – I rather think it's broken.

RATTY *peers down into Mole End*

RATTY:              Oh my lord. How *could* they.

RATTY *makes his stand, approaches* WEASEL

RATTY:              How *could* you.

WEASEL *looms over him*

RATTY:              I *said: how could you.*

WEASEL *hisses.* RATTY *doesn't even flinch*

RATTY:              That isn't English. Answer my question.

WEASEL *shrinks away.* RUBY, *unnoticed by the others, goes off in the direction of the Digger*

WEASEL:             All questions will be handled by an operative
                    of WeaselCo in the fullness of time, and I feel
                    sure that –

*The Digger starts up*

WEASEL:             Ah, Slurpex, right on cue, you read my
                    thoughts exactly. Now, I'm having a slight
                    issue here with *molehills, badger setts,* and
                    in particular *rat-holes,* and they all require
                    consolidation – no indeed, *liquidation.* You
                    can start with –

*The Digger stops*

WEASEL:             Slurpex? – I didn't say stop. You want me
                    to do it? Then I'll do it. If I have to get my
                    hands dirty, getting things clean…

*WEASEL goes. We hear the Digger starting up suddenly*

WEASEL:   Slurpex, I didn't say start – I didn't – what
          are you doing – no, stop, I say, I'm a Weasel,
          I'm *THE WEASEL – NO!!!!*

*Weasel-fur, shreds of tailored suit, shreds of catalogue rain down.
RUBY reappears, taking off a yellow hard-hat. The FRIENDS,
oblivious, still clustered sadly around MOLE*

TOAD:     Y'know, chaps, the Mollster can always stay
          at Toad Hall, eh, plenty of room, you know,
          till she finds her feet again.

RATTY:    No. She can have my place.

BADGER:   She's an undergrounder, Rat, I'll dig her a
          nice new room.

TOAD:     Thing is, chaps, it'll sound a bit silly, but I
          was thinking…

RATTY:    Keep it to yourself eh, Toad.

BADGER:   Yes, now is not the time.

TOAD:     But she was always banging on about –

RATTY/BADGER/
RUBY:     *Sshh!*

TOAD:     Comfy chair was here… little table here…

BADGER:   Sit down, Toad.

RATTY:    No, wait – wait – he's right! Yes!
          The fireplace was here!

BADGER:   The little lamp was here – you clever,
          brilliant Toad!

RUBY:     *[To the stricken MOLE.]* Hey little miner, we're
          takin' you home!

*The pan-pipes have slowly built up as this idea has grown. Now they
all play as the FRIENDS restore MOLE's home. BADGER looks beyond*

BADGER:   *Helper and healer, I cheer/ Small waifs in the
          woodland wet,/You shall look on my power at the
          hopeless hour/But then you shall forget…*

*The pan-pipe fade*

BADGER: It passes into words and out of them again. It is hard to catch, and grows each minute fainter. It plays when it can hear your heartbeat, to tell you its heart is beating too. Then it's gone again, like it never was, like the soft wind in the willows, and it is as if Time itself showed mercy to its creatures, for it let the best deeds be done, and the worst undone.

*MOLE wakes and finds herself at home with her FRIENDS, serving tea*

RATTY: What a capital little house this is! Jolliest place I was ever in, no wonder you're so fond of it...

MOLE: And here's where my picture goes, my mam and dad, they looked after me in the old days –

BADGER: Very handsome couple!

RUBY: Do you need some help with the tea, love?

MOLE: Oh no thank you Ruby I'm fine –

RUBY: Go and help her with the tea, Toad.

TOAD: Well I *would*, old girl, but I've an Announcement to make...

BADGER: Not another speech, Toad, please.

TOAD: No, but I did have some cards made, here, if you look, gold and blue lettering, only the best.

MOLE: *Change of Address...*

TOAD: Well the old, um, *girl*, and me we were chatting in the woods and we thought we might, well –

RUBY: Downsize.

TOAD: Just a tad, no?

| | |
|---|---|
| BADGER: | '*Mr Toad & Miss Boxall, The Gatehouse, Toad Hall.*' But the Gatehouse is a *single room,* Toad. |
| TOAD: | Well yes, but when we sit it'll be a sitting-room, when we dine it'll be a dining-room, and when we go to bed, er – |
| RUBY: | We'll cross that pond when we come to it. |
| BADGER: | But what about Toad Hall? |
| TOAD: | Oh you mean – The Toad Academy! |
| RUBY: | Toad that's not what we agreed. |
| TOAD: | Oh all right. The, er, Academy. |
| RUBY: | A Residential House of Learning For All Creatures Great and Small. Headmistress: Mrs Badger. |
| BADGER: | I beg your pardon? |
| RUBY: | Look we done you a badge, you can't back out now. |
| BADGER: | You know I do believe I'm coming out of retirement… |
| RUBY: | Better get a move on, look! |

*The ACADEMY in full swing. HOB and JILL in smart new uniforms*

| | |
|---|---|
| HOB: | But what if I wanna go home? |
| JILL: | You can't go home, you *are* home! |
| HOB: | I know but I'm also at school, and it's *fun* – it's doing me head in! |

*POOL comes, a teacher*

| | |
|---|---|
| POOL: | Volunteers for Chalk Monitor? |
| HOB/JILL: | Me! Me! |
| POOL: | Both of you? We'll have to have an election! Policies, pundits, polls, speeches, *YESSS!!!* |

*LEAST and VENKY are new teachers*

LEAST: So let me get this straight, if one of my pupils passes a test I get a bonus, right?

VENKY: Er, no mate, not in this game.

LEAST: But hasn't that pupil gotta pay out on my investment?

VENKY: No mate, it just makes you feel good.

LEAST: Hang on, so how do I make money out of this teaching racket?

VENKY: Let's run through it again, mate…

*SIP is the school cook, ERVIN in a smart uniform*

ERVIN: Miss, miss, what's for lunch, miss?

SIP: Today I'll be attempting steak hâché en petit baguette avec frites française –

ERVIN: Burger and chips, yay!

SIP: Avec la sauce de tomate –

ERVIN: Ketchup yay!

*BOXALL, the caretaker*

BOXALL: I do not think this is superb. I'm allowed to stop people goin' into rooms but not allowed to lock 'em in. Reckon I'll just jangle my keys and look grumpy then. And what are *you* doin' here, Toad?

*DORIS, school matron*

DORIS: I 'ave 'opes, I 'ave dreams! I'm gonna maintain 'ealth an' safety standards! I'm gonna administer medicine in line with industry protocols! I'm gonna be the greatest school matron of my day!

*The ACADEMY sets off to start work*

RATTY: Look – I really hate to put the old damper on all this jollity, but I'm awfully afraid I'm… I'm off.

MOLE: Wh-wh-what?

RATTY:      I've – been thinking about it for a while.

MOLE:       Ratty no, no!

RATTY:      See the world and all that, see the sea and so on, always meant to. 'Fraid I'm not much cop at the old goodbyes, so I'll just, I'll just be… well.

*RATTY walks out. Shocked silence. But RATTY's forgotten his suitcase*

RATTY:      Er, not much cop at the old dramatic exits either, if I could just, ah, there we go…

BADGER:     On a Sunday? You're travelling on a *Sunday*?

RATTY:      Oh is it Sunday? Oh…

BADGER:     You know what the trains are like on a Sunday, Rat.

RATTY:      Diabolical, yes. Well I suppose I *could* put the plan on hold for a day or so…

MOLE:       Yes, Ratty, oh a week, a month, forever!

TOAD:       World'll still be out there, eh Ratster?

BADGER:     World's right here, my friend, look around you.

MOLE:       Oh it's a day for messing about in boats!

BADGER:     That newspaper's not going to read itself…

TOAD:       *I* think it's a day for a bit of a *brm-brm-brm* –

RUBY:       No it isn't.

TOAD:       No it isn't.

RATTY:      I believe, when all's said and done, that it is quite the day for a picnic.

MOLE:       Oh yes! But I've no food in the house!

RATTY:      Well, as luck would have it, I took a few supplies for the journey, nothing much really, just a spot of cold chicken cold tongue cold ham cold beef pickled gherkins sausage rolls potted meat cress sandwiches ginger beer fondant fancies chocolate oranges green tictacs port wine prosecco –

*RATTY's suitcase spills picnic things everywhere when suddenly –*

WEASEL: Stop right there!

*WEASEL, thoroughly dishevelled from his fight with the Digger*

WEASEL: It ain't over till I say it's over! ... All right it's over.

*The COMPANY sing*

ALL: *Row row row row*
*Gently gently gently*
*Row your row your row your row your*
*Merrily merrily merrily*

*Life is a long lie-in in the rain*
*Life is a curious face on a train*
*Life is a window opening wide*
*Life is whoever you're sitting beside*
*Life is elevenses, life is tea*
*Life is whatever you're saying to me*
*Life is the two of us painting a room*
*And all of it fits in an afternoon*

*Row row row row*
*Gently gently gently*
*Row your row your row your row your*
*Merrily merrily merrily*

*Life is a million marks on a wall*
*Life is a-dabbling up tails all*
*Life is a sshh and life is a scream*
*And the one thing it isn't it isn't a dream*

*Row row row row*
*Gently gently gently*
*Row your row your row your row your*
*Merrily merrily merrily merrily ROW!*

\*

MERLIN AND THE WOODS OF TIME

*for Alex Clifton, Cestrian*

# Dramatis Personae

## THE WOOD

WATERCUP

an itinerant healer

LILY

his best friend and helper

ELAINE

the Lady of The Woods

## CAMELOT

KING ARTHUR

QUEEN GUINEVERE

SIR LANCELOT

SIR GAWAIN

and

SIR MORDRED

Knights

SIR LUCAN

and

SIR BORS

former Knights, now Experts

HERALD

a singer

MERLIN

THE WHITE KNIGHT

MRS GORMAN

a service professional

## NOTE ON LILY

Lily communicates in two ways, indicated by typography:

1. She mimes, <u>and other characters interpret aloud what she means.</u>

2. Or she mimes and simultaneously speaks the line in Welsh, as printed.

*Merlin and the Woods of Time* was first performed on July 14th 2011 in Grosvenor Park, Chester, as part of the open-air summer season produced by Chester Performs. The play was staged in repertory with *As You Like It* by William Shakespeare.

*Cast*

Nick Asbury – BORS
Mike Burnside – GAWAIN
Paul-Ryan Carberry – LANCELOT
Rob Compton – THE WHITE KNIGHT
Natalie Grady – MRS GORMAN
David Hartley – WATERCUP
Rosie Jones – ELAINE
Alan McMahon – MERLIN
Tarek Merchant – MUSICIAN
Robert Mountford – MORDRED
David Ricardo-Pearce – HERALD
Sophie Roberts – GUINEVERE
Sevan Stephan – ARTHUR
Rebecca Smith Williams – LILY
Andrew Westfield – LUCAN

*Creative Team*

Alex Clifton – Director
takis – Designer
David Shrubsole – Composer
Kay Magson – Casting

With thanks to Rebecca Smith Williams and Angharad Fflur Dafydd for the mystical wood-warble.

# ACT ONE

HERALD:     *Once in the woods of a world you know*
            *A story grew where the lime-trees grow*
            *And it grew till you sat where you sit right now*
            *Between a first word and a final bow*
            *And when it was over, I heard it cry*
            *'Why are we stopping?' Don't ask me why…*

*WATERCUP and LILY. WATERCUP sits, exhausted. LILY signs to him.*

WATERCUP:   Why are we stopping…Don't ask me why,
            Lily, I can't walk any more, we've walked
            since doomsday afternoon is what it feels like.
            How can we eat if we stop…We have no food,
            no money… I *know* we need
            a place of many people, I *know* we need
            a crowd to sell our medicines to, I *know*
            you're hungry, but I'm starving! I'm fading…
            illusions of some great celestial picnic
            swim before my eyes… Lily, I fear
            we've come to the very heart of the wild north-west,
            a place of ghosts and vagabonds, outcasts
            staring vacantly ahead, I seem to…
            see them in my dreams…
LILY:           Ni'n mynd y ffordd anghywir,
            ni angen mynd y ffordd na! [1]
WATERCUP:       Now you make your sad
            nonsensical word-music…
LILY:               Cymraeg fi'n
            siarad, ffwl! [2]

---

[1]     We're going the wrong way,
        we need to go that way!
[2]     I'm speaking Welsh, you fool!

WATERCUP:            Stay with me, poor Lily,
                    be not lost to madness…

LILY:                O Iesu Grist… [3]

WATERCUP:     I fear the lamp of reason dims, for I seem
                    to hear love's music carried on the breeze…

*We hear the voice of ELAINE.*

ELAINE:             *The woods are wide, Sir Dum-de-dum*
                    *The path is only narrow,*
                    *Still I abide, Sir Dum-de-dum*
                    *In my abiding sorrow…*

WATERCUP:     Oh Lily, are we dreaming?

*ELAINE comes, oblivious to them, reading a poem from her commonplace-book.*

ELAINE:             *The woods are big, Sir Dum-de-dum*
                    *And I am only little,*
                    *But yet I love, Sir Dum-de-dum*
                    *Without any…requittle. No…*
                    *I whistle like a kettle?* No!

WATERCUP:    *And Love rides into battle?*

ELAINE:             Who are you? Help!
                 Woodland folk! Somebody help!

WATERCUP:     O Lady
                 Poetical, in your most leafy beauty,
                 a-walking in your lovely bower – I mean
                 leafy bower and lovely beauty –

ELAINE:             A troll!
                 A troll in the wood! In human form, a troll!
                 I am in distress! I need a Knight!

WATERCUP:     May your most
                 holy pardon be most wholly begged
                 by your humble servant.

[3]     Oh Jesus Christ…

ELAINE:          This troll has mastered English.
                 He has a familiar! *(To LILY.)* Were you once a cat?
                 Can he change you back?

WATERCUP:        This is my sister, Lily.
                 She's not my sister but she's like a sister.
                 I've known her since the day I found myself
                 abandoned on the forest trail.

ELAINE:          Do I look
                 as if I care? Why can't she speak?

WATERCUP:        Her mind
                 is gone, she has no words.

LILY:            Fi'n dod o Gymru,
                 y twpsyn! [4]

WATERCUP:        She makes those lovely sounds
                 as if they had a meaning, it's some secret
                 language of the dell perhaps, a tongue
                 known only to the cuckoos.

ELAINE:          Or the trolls!
                 Is she putting a spell on me?

WATERCUP:        (Lily!) We're not
                 trolls, we are travellers. Your exquisite poem,
                 lady, was most pleasing to the ear.
                 I have heard of many knights and their noble exploits
                 in love and battle, but Sir – Dum-de-dum –
                 is not a name I know. Do you mean Sir Dum
                 *of* Dum?

ELAINE:          Fool, I am destined –
                 as I know from a dream I have, a dream in which
                 a golden book falls open to reveal
                 a name so bright I have to shield my eyes –
                 where was I?

WATERCUP:        Destined.

---

[4]    I come from Wales, you idiot!

ELAINE:                    Destined yes, I am destined
            to be the lady of a gallant Knight
            whose name is of three parts, so, 'dum-de-dum'
            I write for now. One day I will fill that space
            with the noble name of my love, but – what is she saying?

*LILY is pointing her fingers down her throat.*

WATERCUP:   Well, she's – saying how very sorry she is
            that God has struck her dumb, for, otherwise,
            she'd cry your loveliness throughout the world.

ELAINE:     Hm. Why does she lift two fingers?

WATERCUP:          That's to tell me –
            she wishes you and she – were close as sisters.

ELAINE:     I'm sure she does but it probably won't happen.
            She being a troll of the woods and I a lady.

WATERCUP:   (Lily, stop.)

ELAINE:          I have no time for this!
            I am bound for the Chapel of Sir Groevanor,
            hard by which Chapel I shall see the Knights
            of Camelot contest the Champion's Shield!
            And there, my dreams inform me,
            will my true love be triumphant.

WATERCUP:   I – too am bound for the Chapel of – that place
            you said, I too shall enter the glorious Lists
            for the glory of – my cause.

ELAINE:          What cause is that then?

WATERCUP:   A noble cause! I shall mount my steed –

ELAINE:          Where's he then?

WATERCUP:   He, um – feedeth in the forest.

ELAINE:          You're not a Knight!
            You look like the weedy boy who makes the shoes
            for the weedy man who stoops to take the heel
            of the weediest Knight to mount his weedy horse.
            By which I mean you're nobody.

WATERCUP:          I'm nobody
            you know.

ELAINE: I know the names
of all the gallant Knights. What's your name?

WATERCUP: My name?

ELAINE: Sir Nobody.

WATERCUP: No, no –

ELAINE: Sir Bootsole.

WATERCUP: No!

ELAINE: Sir Wipe-the-Stable-Clean.

WATERCUP: I am
the Knight – the Knight of…the Tree.

ELAINE: The Knight of the Tree. Which tree.

WATERCUP: That one.

ELAINE: That one.
What, do you live in that tree.

WATERCUP: I pledge *allegiance*
to it.

ELAINE: You pledge allegiance to that tree.

WATERCUP: To the tree, the wood, to all things in nature,
the hills and dales, the winter mist, the summer skies,
the birds, bees, butterflies, the, er, the badgers.

ELAINE: You pledge allegiance to the badgers.

WATERCUP: All things!
From the eagle lofty on his – lofty bough,
down to the meanest ant or earthworm.

ELAINE: Eeuw.

WATERCUP: I am the Knight of All Things God made.

ELAINE: So you couldn't find a Lady to be Knight of.

WATERCUP: No. Well not till now.

ELAINE: Not till now?
What's *now* got that *back then* didn't have?
Has something stopped the world while we weren't looking?
You have no Lady, and you are no Knight.
It's all so sad it's funny, then in fact
so funny it's sad again. Well I leave you, troll,
and your ginger cat you turned to a ginger fool,

and your noble steed invisible,

and your best friends the weeds. I bid you good day.

*ELAINE leaves. WATERCUP enthralled.*

WATERCUP: Good day…good day…So is the sun a firefly.

So is the sea a teardrop. Good day?

Can ever voice have understated so?

Good day – the day against which all my days

are leaves that fall, by other leaves concealed!

LILY: Dilyna hi! [5]

WATERCUP:         Good day – the – what do you mean?

LILY: Mae'n gwybod y ffordd, mae'n mynd lle ma na bobol!

Twrnament! Allwn ni weithio na a neud arian! [6]

WATERCUP: *Go after her!* Of course! Follow my heart!

O sister, in your simple way, you too

point me to my destiny! A good day?

A day that *lasts* for good, that lasts forever!

To the Chapel of Sir Groevanor!

*WATERCUP strides off after Elaine. LILY follows with all their things. Music. Processional. The COURT OF CAMELOT arrives: a HERALD with the Champion's Shield; KING ARTHUR and QUEEN GUINEVERE; SIR LANCELOT, SIR GAWAIN and SIR MORDRED; SIR LUCAN and SIR BORS, bearing the great yellow book WISDOM'S ALMANACK; ELAINE, and ATTENDANTS. They pass through to the Tournament behind. WATERCUP and LILY arrive in time to see the end of the Procession. LUCAN and BORS take up position in the 'puppet tent'. Slits in the back allow them to watch the Lists, before turning to replay the action to us.*

LUCAN: Welcome, riff-raff of the Realm of Arthur,

to the Chapel of Sir Groevanor, for the Great

Tournament of the Champions' Shield. Now it's true

we all have to tighten our belts – we don't but *you* do –

---

[5]    Follow her!

[6]    She knows the way, she's going where there's people.
A tournament! We can work there and make money!

so you can't afford a ringside seat like *we* can,

but this is the next best thing, the very latest

in bringing the action home. These thrilling jousts

by the use of cutting-edge hand-puppetry,

will be broadly cast by us to you. You are watching...

BORS:              Sir Lucan!

LUCAN:                    Lucan for *Love*...

Sir Bors!

BORS:                    Bors for England.

LUCAN:              Lucan for Love and Bors for England. Bors,

talk us through the morning.

BORS:                    Thank you, Lucan.

Three bouts this morning, Tilting With The Lance.

Sir Lancelot of the Lake is in the lists,

we'll see Gawain, and Mordred is a starter.

The going is soft-to-gullible, it would favour

chargers over cold-bloods. Lancelot

has got to be in with a shout, having despatched

Sir Percival in the joust-a-plaisance

at York on Whitsuntide.

LUCAN:                    You could cut the air

with a knife at the end of the day.

BORS:                    Very much so.

Let's look at the form-book, Lucan.

LUCAN:                    Go for it, Bors.

*BORS looks in WISDOM'S ALMANACK; LUCAN looks out at the Lists. LILY is doing*
*all the work setting up their stall, while WATERCUP paces about.*

WATERCUP:    *Good day, good day,* did you hear she bade me *good day*?

Then I saw her in the procession, did you see there,

she beamed right at me, Lily! What are you saying?

<u>I think – that tree – just winked at me...</u> stop it Lily!

I mean it – look, a four-leaf clover! Fortune

favours me! But this will reveal her heart!

She loves me...She loves me not...

oh heavens, the suspense…she…oh.

Stupid folklore. Why would you believe that?

*LUCAN sees WATERCUP pouring out cups of water.*

LUCAN:     Oi, peasant, fetch us a water cup!

WATERCUP:     On its way, sir,

but my name is actually –

LUCAN:     A water cup, I'm thirsty!

*ELAINE arrives, on her way to the Ladies' Convenience.*

ELAINE:     Watercup? Is your name *Watercup*?

WATERCUP:     No he *asked* for a water cup, my name –

LUCAN: *(To ELAINE.)* Hello sweetheart,

you can serve me any time…

ELAINE: *(To WATERCUP.)* This is your job?

You run around and pour out cups of water.

Cups of water – *Watercup*! That's amazing,

your name's just like your job!

WATERCUP: *(Serving LUCAN.)* No, let me explain –

ELAINE:     You pour out water, near to a ladies' toilet.

For the birds and bees and badgers! This is so funny.

WATERCUP:     I am a healer, actually, and I serve

cooling drinks to the knights.

LUCAN:     Enough water, lad,

fetch us a jug of wine!

WATERCUP:     Yes, sir.

LUCAN: *(To ELAINE.)*     D'you fancy

a stiffener, sweetheart? Think we've met before…

BORS:     Here come the Knights, Sir Lucan!

*LUCAN turns his attention to the Lists, as WATERCUP serves him and BORS.*

ELAINE:     Watercup, who fetches cups of water.

WATERCUP:     At least my name has three parts. Dum-de-dum.

ELAINE:     That may be so but it's not *Sir* Watercup,

is it?

WATERCUP:     It shall be some day.

ELAINE:  Shall it really.

WATERCUP:  Watercup was I named on the day I met you.
Watercup shall I be.

ELAINE:  How interesting.

WATERCUP:  One day you shall see me fight in a noble cause
against impossible odds, and for a lady.

ELAINE:  Some lady who's in want of a cup of water?
I'm not. I'm not in want of a Knight at all.
I have found one. I saw him from afar.
His standard is of azure-blue and his name
is of three parts. As is his character,
for he is brave, sweet, honourable, and – four parts.
Noble, honourable, handsome, brave – five parts.
Handsome, noble, sweet – oh the joust is starting!

*A drum-roll, and ELAINE runs out. WATERCUP notices Wisdom's Almanack.*

WATERCUP:  She has found her Knight? Then I have found my night-time.
Still, hope grows where nothing grows. What *is* this
book they treat like treasure…
'Wisdom's Almanack…The Guide Compleat
to Chivalry, Its Codes and Exemplars…
Once, on the Field of Claverton, Sir Wimbold
in the sable colours of the Lady Belgrave
hath Tempered the Sword of Justice three times
with Humanity and Mercy… At Yuletide
on the Field of Christleton, Sir Mickle Trafford
Hath righteously defended the Good Name
Of Lady Hoole, Lady Wervin, Lady Foregate,
and Lady Chorlton-by-Backford', oh, sweet ladies,
noble Sir Mickle Trafford! *(He daydreams.)* In August,
on the field of – Groevanor, Sir Watercup
hath rode in the colours of the Lady – what?
I don't know her name!

LILY: Der ma a blydi helpa fi! [7]

*WATERCUP puts the book down and goes back to the stall.*

WATERCUP: Sorry, Lily, you're right, we have our work,
we brew, we serve, we heal, and so we live.
For sure, in this Almanack you'll read no record
of Sir Watercup. But I wonder…if I read that,
then I would know what *they* know…

*A trumpet sounds.*

LUCAN: And we're off!
Gawain in green, Mordred in jet-black…
Gawain is riding Winalot, his warmblood
charger, while Sir Mordred's on No-Hoper…
Gawain is aiming high, Mordred low,
it's going to be one or the other, that's jousting,
and bang and Mordred's off, he's down, Gawain
has taken it, wham-bam, that'll do nicely,
blood on the grass, we like it there, goodnight
and so to Bedivere. I'm Lucan for Love.

BORS: And I'm Bors for England. Lancelot's next up.

WATERCUP: Lily, I have got to get that book.
I *know* the disgusting man and the boring man
are using it, but look it's so gigantic
it must be the only copy on God's earth.
And it could turn me to the Knight I know
I'm destined to become!

HERALD: A water cup!

*MORDRED comes, covered in blood, supported by the HERALD. LILY assesses his injuries and signs to WATERCUP.*

WATERCUP: Ruptured spleen, cracked rib, internal bleeding,
indigestion, scurvy, halitosis,
earache, anger issues…That's a florin.

[7]   Come here and bloody help me!

*MORDRED pays.* LILY *and* WATERCUP *help him into their tent*

LUCAN:     Hey Bors, you know a little bird just told me
the Passage-of-Arms is to be judged today
by Queen Guinevere.

BORS:            That's a first in jousting,
Lucan, that's extraordinary.

LUCAN:            A *lady*
judging on the tilts? Do me a favour.
How can she know the rule on strikes?

BORS:            Chivalric
correctness gone mad. I'm Bors for England.

LUCAN:     I'm Lucan for Love. Now, don't get me wrong,
that Guinevere can judge me on *my* tilts
any time she likes, eh…

BORS:            That's a good one.
That's a good use of humour.

*They go to the Convenience.* WATERCUP *emerges from the healing tent.*

WATERCUP:  Look, they're taking a break, this is my chance…
Lily, bandage him up, it's now or never!

*He runs to the puppet tent, lifts up the Almanack, stuffs it under his shirt and
creeps back to the healing tent, from which* MORDRED *emerges.*

WATERCUP:  How are you feeling, sir?

MORDRED:         Ninety-seven
jousts. Ninety-six defeats. One draw.
*Get in there!* I shall build on that. One day
God willing I shall draw again. On that day
Camelot shall know the name of…Mordred.

WATERCUP:  I think they know your name. You're the one who always
loses.

MORDRED:         Wrong. Not always. Once, in Lincoln,
I fell from my horse, but…*so did my opponent.*
It had never happened before, but…now it's happened.
D'you see? D'you see the pattern?

*MORDRED goes. LILY emerges. LUCAN and BORS return to their tent.*

WATERCUP: *(To LILY.)* Go round, creep about, find out the lady's name.
<u>What am *I* going to do</u>? Read this book.

*LILY goes. The trumpet sounds. BORS watches the joust, LUCAN relays it.*

BORS: Off they go, the second bout of the morning,
and for those of you watching this in sable-and-argent,
Gawain's in vert, Lancelot's in azure
and bang!

LUCAN: That's got to hurt.

BORS: Gawain is off!

LUCAN: Wham-bam-Bedivere, blood on the grass,
that's jousting! There's a lady in the stands
swooning with emotion, look she's down,
it's another conquest for Sir Lancelot!

BORS: And *that* is very much your department,
the ladies, very much a colourful
sideshow to the action.

LUCAN: That was her,
*thought* I knew her, the Lady of The Woods...
Looks like she's got the hots for Lancelot.
That's not going to please the Queen eh, Bors?

BORS: Indeed.
– Why's that?

LUCAN: Why's that? The Queen and Lancelot?
You spent the last few months alone in a cave?

BORS: Er, yes, I did.

LUCAN: The Lady of The Woods, eh...
What *is* that lady's name?

*LILY has come back and is signing letters for WATERCUP.*

WATERCUP: <u>Egg</u> – E, <u>Lip</u> – L, <u>Arse</u> – A, <u>Eye</u> – I,
<u>Nose</u> – N, <u>Elbow</u> – E. That's her name? –
Arseline? Go back a bit. Eglaine?
Eglantine? Elaine! Elaine! What else?

She <u>threw</u> – she threw her <u>favour</u>…for me?
No no, what am I thinking, for one of the knights,
the – <u>long knight</u>, long, oh <u>a long lance</u>,
Sir Lance – <u>a bit? A lot!</u> Sir Lance-a-lot?
<u>She threw…her favour to Sir Lancelot</u>. Oh.

*Poor* WATERCUP. *The* HERALD *drags in* GAWAIN.

| | |
|---|---|
| HERALD: | We need a water cup! |
| WATERCUP: | That's me! |
| HERALD: | Gawain. |
| GAWAIN: | Blast ye Lancelot, yer silver-tongued slim-waisted cool bilingual metrosexual fairy! |

LILY *assesses him and signals,* WATERCUP *makes notes.*

| | |
|---|---|
| WATERCUP: | <u>Burst liver, ruptured kidneys,</u> lance envy (lance envy? that's a new one), <u>lumbago, runny nose</u>. That's three florins. |

*The* HERALD *finds some coins on* GAWAIN *and pays. They drag him into the healing tent. The* HERALD *departs.* WATERCUP *goes back to the Almanack.*

| | |
|---|---|
| WATERCUP: | You do it, Lily, I'm busy. |
| LILY: | Darllen llyfr? [8] |
| WATERCUP: | Yes reading a book, a book that could change our lives! |
| LILY: | Bu ti byth yn farchog! [9] |
| WATERCUP: | I *will* be a knight, I'll best all-comers and win my lady's hand! One day I shall fight for her in a noble cause! |
| LILY: | Anghofia'r fenyw dwp! [10] |
| WATERCUP: | I *can't* forget the stupid la – she's not a stupid lady! |

[8]   Reading a book?

[9]   You'll never be a knight!

[10]   Forget the stupid lady!

She is the Lady Elaine. And I can't forget her.

What do you mean I'm <u>reading it upside-down</u>?

How would you know, you can't even read the words.

LILY:      Diw e ddim yn gymraeg! [11]

WATERCUP:        Your mystical wood-warble...

O, my love for Elaine makes all sounds
melodious.

GAWAIN:        Get yer ragged arse in here,

yer parasitic paramedic vulture!

*LILY goes back in. WATERCUP slowly turns the Almanack upside down, as LUCAN
and BORS realise it's missing.*

LUCAN:      Aye-aye, where's Wisdom gone? That yellow tome

we always heave about to look important.

BORS:      It was right there on the plinth.

LUCAN:        Well who cares.

I never read it anyway.

BORS:        Nor me.

I know it off by heart, like you.

LUCAN:        Like me?

Books, old lad? Books are for girls. Chin-chin.

*They drink. Drum-roll at the Tournament. WATERCUP gazes at the pictures.*

WATERCUP:      Mysterious sketches scribbled in the margins...

portending what? Ingredients
for a liquid red in colour...but this picture
shows the sun at dawn and then at twilight...
then all four seasons side-by-side, and stars
that fly away like birds...what *is* this potion?
And here's another, elements of a compound
blue in colour. Here though, in these pictures
the sun sits in the selfsame place...*always*...

[11]    It's not in Welsh!

*The trumpet sounds.*

LUCAN: We're off, to the left in black on his dark horse
the dark horse, the underdog, Mordred,
against the azure blue of the ladies' choice
Sir Lancelot of the Lake. This could be ugly –
as the bishop said at the door of the witch's chamber –
and Lancelot's gone high and Mordred midward
and bang they're in, knock-knock, and Mordred's gone
and he's lost his head for keeps, it's literally
bouncing, like some bowling-ball of Satan,
into the Royal Box!

BORS: Sir Lancelot
is Champion of the Morning. I can confirm
we have a decapitation.

LUCAN: Aye-aye, look,
Lancelot's in trouble too, it's his hand,
he's took a knock.

BORS: Looks like a fingernail.

LUCAN: Devoted ladies, I know you'll be shocked to hear
the news on that fingernail, we'll keep you posted.
We're Lucan for Love.

BORS: And Bors for England.

WATERCUP: I've cracked it!

*WATERCUP takes the Almanack to LILY, as GAWAIN departs the tent, healed.*

WATERCUP: You drink this red elixir, and it makes
Time go faster…so you can see the future…
you can *see the future*! Why would you want to do that.
Why? Because you'll know what's going to happen!
Why would you want to know that. Why, because –
you'll have the power to change it! Why would you want
to have that. Look – I don't know – it's, it's a potion!
And this blue elixir makes Time…stand still,
like an antidote…I could use this, I could use this…

to make the lady love me! If she loved me
I would make the world a better place! To work...
Rose-petals, sage, carnation, for the red...
Lilac, hydrangea, bindweed, for the blue...

*MORDRED comes, carrying his head.*

WATERCUP:    Decapitation. That'll be half a crown.
MORDRED:     Are you trying to be funny?

*LANCELOT comes, holding his finger gingerly, taking out his silver wallet.*

LANCELOT:        Woodland people ahoy!
             Damn little bit peeled off here, not very clever.
             A crown for your pains, now cure me, little mice.

*WATERCUP takes the payment; LILY looks at his finger and signs a diagnosis.*

WATERCUP:    <u>Fingernail.</u> And <u>Toffee-nose.</u>
LANCELOT:        What you say there?
WATERCUP:    Nothing, sir. (Lily, it's him, my rival.
             I ought to challenge him, man-to-man! I know,
             I know I <u>have to be true to my healer's oath...</u>)

*LANCELOT goes into the tent. WATERCUP shows LILY a page from the Almanack.*

WATERCUP:    Lily, see these plants? Go to the forest,
             gather them all...take two different baskets,
             mark one red and mark one blue. – Now, sir...

*WATERCUP goes into the tent. LILY signs to MORDRED to wait. She goes into the
tent and returns with a fold-out chair and a copy of HAIL! magazine. MORDRED
sits, his HEAD reading the magazine. LILY goes back into the healing tent, comes
out with two baskets. ELAINE comes by, with her commonplace book.*

ELAINE:      Ah, simple girl, off on some country errand.

*LILY just looks at her. Then she heads into the woods.*

ELAINE:      Oh. You are Sir Mordred, the Black Knight.
             You did very well.
MORDRED:         I would have won on points

|  | but that's not how they judge it, is it. |
|---|---|
| ELAINE: | No… |
| MORDRED: | It's so unfair. I *had* him. |
| ELAINE: | Tell me, Black Knight, |
|  | do you know where they cure the serious injuries? |

*MORDRED gives her a look, as his BODY points at the healing tent.*

| ELAINE: | That *waterboy* is healing Lancelot? |
|---|---|
|  | My knight is in the hands of *Watercup*? |
| MORDRED: | Only cos he's rich. If you're like me |
|  | you have to wait your turn. |
| ELAINE: | I'm not like you. |
|  | I'm the Lady of The Woods, but history |
|  | will sing my name in unison with that |
|  | of Lancelot. |
| MORDRED: | Not according to these pictures. |
|  | Look, he's always standing by the Queen. |
|  | The two of them together. Then the King, |
|  | then behind them, look, there's all these little people. |
| ELAINE: | That's…perspective, Mordred. |
|  | The people are far away, so they look small. |
| MORDRED: | They sent them far away? Because they were small? |
| ELAINE: | Er, no, it's not important – |
| MORDRED: | They're not important? |
|  | Why, because they're small? |
| ELAINE: | Please be quiet. |

*WATERCUP emerges.*

| WATERCUP: | Elaine! You've come to watch me at my work? |
|---|---|
| ELAINE: | You wish. I've come to see if my Champion |
|  | has had his fingernail restored to health. |
| WATERCUP: | I did my best. |
| ELAINE: | Yes well that's your job. |
|  | Now excuse me, I'm in love and you're in the way. |

*ELAINE goes into the tent. WATERCUP sighs.*

WATERCUP:    Sir Mordred, I will see you
for free this time and every time. I believe
good health should be a public service.

MORDRED:    Do you.
And the small people out there, I don't suppose
that applies to the small people.

WATERCUP:    What small people.

MORDRED:    They were sent away, you can't see them.

WATERCUP:    Ri-ight… In return,
will you help me test a couple of new products
and ask no questions of me?

MORDRED:    I'm your man.

WATERCUP:    It's really just a red drink and a blue drink.

*LANCELOT and ELAINE emerge from the tent. LILY comes from the woods with her baskets full, and goes in, followed by WATERCUP and MORDRED.*

ELAINE:    What do you think of the poem, Sir Lancelot?

LANCELOT:    Oh? Tremendous. Love the way it rhymes
here and there, and then, doesn't. Cracking stuff.

ELAINE:    It's about a gallant knight, it's a poem of love
for the bravest knight in the world!

LANCELOT:    That's tremendous.

ELAINE:    It's about how a lady loves him, and one day,
at a Tournament, across a crowded greensward,
he notices this lady and their eyes meet,
and he falls in love with her.

LANCELOT:    Oh that's cracking stuff.
I like a good yarn!

ELAINE:    No it's based on real life.

LANCELOT:    Is it, now. Real life, eh. Dum-de-dum…
Don't reckon I've met the blighter.
Is he one of the Lancashire Dum-de-dums? Well now,
I wouldn't say no to a crack at him.

ELAINE:    It's you!
*You* are Sir Dum-de-dum! The verse was written

by the lady who's in love with you, and the girl
you fall in love with wrote the lines, and *I* –
am the writer of the poem!

LANCELOT:     Slow down there,
that's three whole different ladies.

ELAINE:     No it's not!
Take out Sir Dum-de-dum and in its place
say Lancelot!

LANCELOT:     You want me to take the place
of Dum-de-dum? He won't take that lying down.

ELAINE:     There *is* no Dum-de-dum!

LANCELOT:     So he died in battle?
Saves me the trouble, eh!

*GUINEVERE comes by and sees ELAINE.*

GUIN:     Oh look, a fan club.
Is the Queen allowed to join?

LANCELOT:     Look here, Guin, it's a poem
this little lady's done. It's about
real life. There's these three gorgeous fillies
all vying for this fellow Dum-de-dum,
but then he's slain in combat, and all Lancashire's
in mourning. Damn, I gave away the ending.

*GUINEVERE snatches the poem.*

GUIN:     *The woods are wide, Sir Dum-de-dum*
*The path is only narrow,*
*Still I abide, Sir Dum-de-dum*
*My heart pierced by Love's arrow...*
It's crap. I need a drink. Where'd you find this?
*(Sees ELAINE.)* Oh, hello, is it yours? It's very good.
But I never heard of this Dum-de-dum.

LANCELOT:      Passed away,
               rest his soul. Bit of a star.
ELAINE:        No – no –
               it's just a space for any knight whose name
               is in three parts.
LANCELOT:      Tremendous.
GUIN:                   You mean syllables?
LANCELOT:      Hang on, well, *Lance*, that's one. *Lance-a*, that's two…er…
               this poetry lark is pretty technical, no?
GUIN:                   *The woods are big, Sir* – Hobbyhorse
                        *And I am only small,*
                        *But yet I love, Sir* – Marmalade
                        *As long as the leaves fall.*
                        *The sky is blue, Sir* – Bellyflop**,** this is fun!
LANCELOT:      You show grave disrespect to the memory
               of brave Sir Dum-de-dum, my dear.
GUIN:                   Do I really.
LANCELOT:      You do.
GUIN:               I do.
LANCELOT:               You do.
GUIN:                        I do, do I?
               Do you?
LANCELOT:           I do.
GUIN:                    I do.
LANCELOT:                    I do.
ELAINE:                           Excuse me,
               your Majesty, um, can I have my poem back?

*GUINEVERE gives the poem back to LANCELOT.*

GUIN:      There, my love, you can blow your nose in springtime.

*LANCELOT gives it back to ELAINE and wraps her hand round it.*

LANCELOT:      You keep that safe, little lady,
               in memory of Sir Dum-de-dum, a good man
               who fell in the field, the pride of Lancashire.

*GUINEVERE and LANCELOT go. ELAINE follows. MORDRED emerges from the tent, fully recovered, with a bottle of Red Elixir. WATERCUP and LILY follow, WATERCUP still studying the pictures, LILY carrying a bottle of the Blue Elixir.*

WATERCUP:    Now, this red one makes Time fly…
and the blue one makes Time stand still… Oh Lily,
the power to alter Time…
What are you asking me? <u>Will I use that power</u>
<u>responsibly…or like a complete</u> – Lily,
that's just not acceptable signage.
I will use my power for Love, as a Knight should do!

MORDRED:    So I drink this?

WATERCUP:        Just a sip, just to try it…

*MORDRED drinks the Red Elixir. Strange trill of music.*

WATERCUP:    What do you feel?

MORDRED:        Nothing.

LILY:            Wast o amser! [12]

MORDRED:    Nothing at all but…*rage*, murderous rage!
That the House of Uther and this upstart villain Arthur
should sit on the throne while I, the spawn of Evil,
slouch in the gutters! But I shall bide my time,
bear the blows, endure the humiliation,
for the day will come when I will rise to power,
and the Small People will rise, and in their name
I shall put this Realm to the sword. Blood shall foam
in every forest, corpses shall be strewn
like mown grass on each village green, for I
am Mordred, nemesis of Camelot,
nightmare of all England!

WATERCUP:    Don't…drink any more just yet.
– Lily, the antidote –

*LILY passes WATERCUP the Blue Elixir.*

[12]    Waste of time!

WATERCUP:          All that evil
                   has probably made you thirsty, try this.

MORDRED:           Is it the souls of my enemies?

WATERCUP:          Er…yes.

*MORDRED drinks the Blue Elixir, a strange opposing trill.*

MORDRED:           I mean to – I mean I need to – I need to…
                   I need to do some work on my jousting.
                   Then I'll be the best…well…better, can't win 'em all.
                   Did I tell you what happened at Lincoln?
                   I fell from my horse. But so did my opponent.

*WATERCUP takes the Blue Elixir away and MORDRED walks away.*

WATERCUP:          It works, he flew to the future – then he came back!
                   That must be Mordred's destiny, he'll become
                   the Enemy of the Realm, did you hear him ranting?
                   The red one makes Time fly!
                   The blue one makes Time slow down to nothing…
                   Elaine believes she's destined to be loved
                   by Lancelot… and, if she drank the red,
                   then that would come true… but what if she drinks the blue?
                   She'll be…stupid for eternity she's not stupid!
                   I could keep her here in the present, in the moment,
                   never moving towards her destiny, and I –
                   would have eternity to change her mind!
                   And when she does, and falls in love with me,
                   I shall be the very flower of chivalry –
                   *Sir* Watercup! And if anything goes wrong,
                   we'll use the red as an antidote…To the forest!

*WATERCUP goes into the forest. LILY puts her head in her hands, then follows. Music.*
*The HERALD, with ARTHUR, GUINEVERE and all the KNIGHTS.*

HERALD:  King Arthur and Queen Guinevere of England!
     It is decreed that Sir Lancelot of the Lake
     is Champion of the Morning!
     Please show your appreciation of the great
     Knights of Castle Camelot, past and present!

*LANCELOT, GAWAIN, MORDRED, LUCAN and BORS take applause.*

HERALD:  In celebration of our national sport,
     and recognition of the love and justice
     by which he reigns in England, King Arthur
     and his Queen will distribute alms to his poorer subjects.

*ARTHUR and GUINEVERE distribute food to the audience. The HERALD sings.*

HERALD:     *What will be*
         *What will be*
         *Clambering into the apple tree*
         *Gazing down at the glittering town*
         *A nobody*
         *What will be*

         *What's to come*
         *What's to come*
         *On the horizon beating a drum*
         *Looking for love or what it's made of*
         *Dum-de-dum*
         *What's to come*

         *What happens now*
         *What happens now*
         *Another deep breath another deep bow*
         *Fight or fly, the light goes by*
         *Any old how*
         *What happens now*

*What has been*
*What has been*
*The sights I've seen and haven't seen*
*Are the same again the moment when*
*I leave the scene*
*What has been*

*What will be*
*What will be*
*Clambering into the apple tree*
*Gazing down at the glittering town*
*A nobody*
*What will be*

ARTHUR: Love, time, and a picnic, what do you say,
try beating that! Good luck! That's the big three,
love, a picnic and yes, what the other one was.

GUIN: Time.

ARTHUR: Waits for no, what, no parsnips, eh?
no flies on them, Time flies, it was only this morning
it feels I was just a nipper –

GUIN: Oh here we go.

ARTHUR: A boy in the woods, the trees, nothing like trees,
try beating trees, you can't! You learn your trade,
king in my case, but in *your* case, well, perhaps,
a humble, sort of, craft-type thing…and in *your* case?
Beggar maybe, with not a care in the world…
Then there's the dreamer there, look, miles away
in the parish of young love…send my regards,
won't you, I used to tend a plot there! Now,
let me guess, I'm good at this…oh, a housewife,
cooking and darning, seeing to all his needs!
Now *you* look thick! I mean thick as thieves, like friends!
and that's a trade of a kind, ask me no questions,
tell me no lies, and so we pass our days,

days and nights and hot and cold and soon
we're older now and young at heart are we not,
old as the woman we feel, so we're young, eh! Dearest…
What next, I forget, you forget, we forget together,
a carnival of forgetting! clouds go by,
and the firelight to come, what do you say!
One day today will be your, your, your heyday.
But you won't know till it's gone and that's a promise!
For all the world is a – what, it's all something, eh,
it's where, where stuff goes on, eh? Oh I *had* it –
can't for the life of me *think* what all the world is!

GUIN:      Thank God for that, we can eat.

LANCELOT:      That's cracking stuff,
Your Majesty.

*Applause. THE KNIGHTS start drinking. LANCELOT spreads a blanket for the Royal picnic. WATERCUP and LILY creep back, each with a basket of plants.*

WATERCUP:      I don't *care* what you think, I am in love,
I don't care what *I* think! I have the power
to alter Time, and, in the name of love
I shall serve my Lady Elaine the Blue Elixir
and preserve her beauty for eternity
in my company.

LILY:      O ti'n yfarch o bidin. [13]

WATERCUP:      I don't even know that sign. I am in love,
sister, there is nothing to be done
but everything!

*WATERCUP and LILY go into the tent.*

ARTHUR:      Lancelot, Champion, join us!

LANCELOT:      I thought perhaps Your Majesties might like
a little time?

---

[13]    Oh you're such a penis.

| | |
|---|---|
| GUIN: | We had our time already. |
| | Sit down, chief. |
| ARTHUR: | The Champion's always welcome |
| | at my table, or my blanket, eh? |
| GUIN: | Especially |
| | welcome in your blanket. |
| ARTHUR: | That's right, |
| | especially at a picnic! But look here, |
| | it's a square blanket,  now there's one whole side |
| | where no one sits! Is there not a guest to join us? |

*ELAINE appears, with her own little picnic things. They see her.*

| | |
|---|---|
| LANCELOT: | Now you mention it – |
| GUIN: | No there's no one. Three for lunch. |
| LANCELOT: | Well look, I can fix it, there: the Round Blanket! |

*LANCELOT fashions the blanket into a circle. ELAINE sets up her own picnic.*

| | |
|---|---|
| ARTHUR: | I say, that's a corking move, now it doesn't feel |
| | like anybody's missing! |
| GUIN: | Nobody's missing. |
| ARTHUR: | The Round Blanket. Not just a Champion |
| | but also a bit of a, what – |
| GUIN: | A dab-hand. Husband, |
| | in recognition of his glorious triumph |
| | I shall weave a tapestry of him, for which purpose |
| | it is essential that I study him |
| | closely and at length. |
| ARTHUR: | Indeed, my dear! |
| | You really are a craftsman! I should say |
| | crafts-*woman* (yes why not) a woman of craft |
| | indeed. You craft away! |
| GUIN: | It is essential |
| | also that I measure his dimensions, |
| | so my work is true to life. |
| ARTHUR: | True to life, eh? |

Bravo, I love to see a master at work!

Or a mistress I should say!

GUIN:            Shut up.

ARTHUR:                Heigh-ho!

*GUINEVERE starts measuring LANCELOT's dimensions, ARTHUR eats his picnic.*

LUCAN:           All right, have we got it down: Gawain goes first.

A minute with the bird. If the bird yields,    *(ELAINE.)*

your booze is free till Christmas, if she doesn't –

who drew second?

GAWAIN:         Damn whoever drew it,

we shan't be needing second.

MORDRED:       I drew second.

LUCAN:           Who drew second?

MORDRED:       I did, I'm right here, lads.

LUCAN:           Was it you, Bors?

BORS:              I drew fourth.

MORDRED:       I DREW SECOND!

LUCAN:           All right, don't rust your armour. I drew third.

Floor is yours, Big G.

*GAWAIN approaches ELAINE.*

GAWAIN:         May I join ye, lass, ye look very down in the mouth.

ELAINE:          It depends how long it is.

GAWAIN:         How long what is?

ELAINE:          Your name.

GAWAIN:         My name's Gawain.

ELAINE:          Not long enough.

*GAWAIN goes back, LUCAN and MORDRED laugh at him.*

GAWAIN:         Typical English lass, she wouldn't know

a real man if it bit her. I was about to

but the timing wasnae right.

LUCAN:           Who drew second?

MORDRED:       I DREW SECOND!

*MORDRED approaches ELAINE.*

MORDRED:      Lady, I am Mordred.

ELAINE:       I know that. Mordred what.

MORDRED:      Mordred – I don't know.

ELAINE:       Go away.

MORDRED:      Right.

*MORDRED goes back, GAWAIN and LUCAN laugh at him.*

MORDRED:      Oh I'm a numbskull!
              I forgot to tell her what happened at Lincoln.

LUCAN:        Shame.
              In the next life, sunshine. My go.

*LUCAN approaches ELAINE.*

LUCAN:        Sweetheart, let me tell you my name, it's long,
              so I'll pour us out some wine, and by and by
              we'll make acquaintance. Now my name in full –

ELAINE:       I know your name, and know you are widely known
              as Lucan of the Little Cock. I presume
              there's a cockerel on your family crest.

LUCAN:        There – is,
              yes, a cockerel, not to scale, but *rampante*,
              sanguine on a field of, er…chevrons.

*LUCAN goes back, deflated. GAWAIN and MORDRED laugh at him. BORS approaches ELAINE. She glares at him, he does a U-turn.*

BORS:         Not my type.

GAWAIN:       Shoulda bitten her.

MORDRED:      Not my sign.

LUCAN:        No sense of humour at all, that one. Chin-chin!

*The KNIGHTS booze together. WATERCUP, with a jug of the Blue Elixir, and LILY come out of the tent.*

WATERCUP:     <u>This is…going to end…in tears.</u> You're right for once!
              Tears of happiness! When she drinks this drink

she'll stay here in the moment forever,
and everything I ever meant to tell her
I'll come to in my *own time!* My lady,
would you care for a glass of wine?

ELAINE:     I would not. I am having a pie.

WATERCUP:         This would go well
with pie.

ELAINE:         Your wine is blue, fool. I would never
drink blue wine.

WATERCUP:         They, brew it in the Chapel,
the, er, the monks.

ELAINE:         I am a Christian.
It's my Christian duty to drink what is made by monks.

WATERCUP:     That's very well put, my lady.

*ELAINE drinks a deep draught of the Blue Elixir.*

WATERCUP:     Lady Elaine? Lady Elaine?
It's working, I can feel it. Now's my time…
Lady Elaine, O Lady of The Woods,
I have loved you since that moment in the forest
when first I did set eyes upon you. Yea,
I am rude and humbly born, and yet my heart
is pure, my soul is true, my troth is plighted.

ELAINE:     Dum.

WATERCUP:         What did you say?

ELAINE:     De dum.

WATERCUP:         Lady Elaine?

ELAINE:     Dum…de dum…I love…

WATERCUP:         Yes? Yes?

ELAINE:     I love…this piece of pie.

WATERCUP:     You love – the piece of pie?

ELAINE:         It is a pie.
Some of a pie. I love it.

WATERCUP:         Good, that's good,
*I* like pie, too, we could talk pie,

couldn't we, have a chat about favourite pies.

ELAINE: I want *this* pie. It is all brown.

WATERCUP: Elaine,

don't look at the pie, look at me.

ELAINE: I love…

WATERCUP: You love – ?

ELAINE: I love the crust of the pie.

WATERCUP: Yes, moving on –

ELAINE: I love the crust of…the crust. Oh. Oh yes.

A ladybird. It is every…thing…I want…

from…a ladybird. Red parts. Black parts.

WATERCUP: Lily! What have I done?

*LILY comes out.*

WATERCUP: My love has become quite boring! <u>What do you mean
'become' quite boring</u> – look, she can't even see me!

*LILY waves her hand in front of ELAINE's eyes.*

ELAINE: Hello fingers… Farewell fingers…

Hello fingers… Farewell fingers…

WATERCUP: Oh God!

The red, the red, we have to make the red!

*WATERCUP and LILY rush back into their tent*

ARTHUR: My Guinevere, my Queen,

the day draws on, daylight, daylong, my dearest,

shall we steal unto our bower?

GUIN: Talk in English.

You're king of where they have to. Yes, let's do it.

Sir Lancelot has become a lover of poems.

He can pun on himself in private.

*GUINEVERE stalks off with ARTHUR. LANCELOT approaches ELAINE.*

LANCELOT: Guess what, finished my homework, done my counting:

Lance-a-lot, three syllables, may I sit?

|  | I'm all yours for a jiffy! How about that? |
|  | Lady? Lady Poet? |
| ELAINE: | Look a white thread. |
|  | Then a gold thread. Then a blue thread. Then a white thread. |
| LANCELOT: | Embroidery your thing, eh? Cracking stuff. |
| ELAINE: | I love the white thread. Look. An ant. |
| LANCELOT: | Oh yes. |
|  | There he goes, little feller. Marvellous. Yes… |
|  | All that aside, I expect you'd like to know |
|  | what it's like to be a Champion! |
| ELAINE: | Hello |
|  | speck of dust. Farewell speck of dust. |
| LANCELOT: | Hmm. Yes. *(To the* KNIGHTS.*)* You boys got any wine left? |
| LUCAN: | We're missing you, lad, get *in* here! |
| GAWAIN: | If ye can spare |
|  | a moment for your friends, ye great big nancy! |

*LANCELOT abandons ELAINE for the livelier KNIGHTS. WATERCUP and LILY come out of the healing tent with jugs of the Red Elixir.*

| WATERCUP: | Keep those there in case we need them… Lady Elaine, how are you feeling? |
| ELAINE: | Feeling… |
|  | Feeling. Fee Ling. Feeeeeeeeeeeeeeeee… |

*LANCELOT raises an empty bottle*

| LANCELOT: | Charming, *that* is! Wait for the Champion, won't you? |
| LUCAN: | The case, Bors! |
| BORS: | We finished the case, it's empty. |
|  | I suggested moderation, but – |
| LUCAN: | Shut it, four-eyes. |
|  | We're out of booze! |
| LANCELOT: | Ridiculous! |
| GAWAIN: | Yer lightweights, |
|  | ye didnae bring enough! |
| MORDRED: | Look over there! |

LANCELOT:    That water-chap, he's got a whole bloody cellar!
             Well spotted, Bors.

MORDRED:            Actually it was me.

LUCAN:       Four-eyes, you saved the day!

MORDRED:            If I could just mention –

GAWAIN:      Boys, it's a Castle-Crawl!

KNIGHTS:            CASTLE-CRAWL!

*The KNIGHTS descend upon WATERCUP's supply of Red Elixir.*

WATERCUP:    Excuse me, it's/not wine –

LANCELOT:           /Good day Sir Beaujolais...
             How now Sir Côtes du Rhône...

WATERCUP:           I say it's not wine,
             it's medicine!

LUCAN:              Then it's going to make me better,
             water-monkey!

*LUCAN pushes WATERCUP over. The KNIGHTS start guzzling the Red Elixir. ARTHUR and GUINEVERE return from the bower.*

ARTHUR:      Oh look, high jinks! Try beating that!

GUIN:               They're drunk.
             They're a disgrace.

ARTHUR:             They are the soul of England,
             the noblest knights of the Kingdom!

*The KNIGHTS have all stopped drinking. They feel strange. The Red Elixir takes effect. LANCELOT runs to GUINEVERE.*

LANCELOT:    Guinevere, you are mine, I can wait no longer!

*He kisses her passionately.*

ARTHUR:      I say, love in abundance, eh, good friends,
             good chums, eh, soul mates, what?

*LUCAN runs to LANCELOT's side, and BORS to ARTHUR's.*

LUCAN:        I am Lucan for Love!
                I will live and die for a Lady! (When I get one.)

BORS:        I will live and die for my King, I am Bors for England!

ARTHUR:    Well thank you, Bors, but let's not take sides.

*GAWAIN squares up to LANCELOT.*

GAWAIN:    Let's not take sides, ye say? *Let's not take sides?*
                This ladies' man is threatening the union
                of honourable knights!

LANCELOT:    Name your weapon,
                ragamuffin.

*MORDRED attempts to take centre stage.*

MORDRED:    It is I, Sir Mordred,
                whom am your Foe. I am the son of –

GUIN:        Crikey,
                I'm having what they're having.

*The KNIGHTS freeze in tense stand-off, as GUINEVERE swigs one of the bottles.*

GUIN:        Stuff England and stuff Camelot, I want you!

*GUINEVERE leaps on LANCELOT and they fall to the ground, writhing.*

ARTHUR:    Shall we take five, perhaps, I think things are getting
                a little Mediterranean here…

MORDRED:    It is I,
                Sir Mordred, who –

GAWAIN:    For real men everywhere!

*GAWAIN hauls LANCELOT up and thumps him. All the KNIGHTS draw daggers.*

LUCAN:        Lucan for Love!

*LUCAN kills GAWAIN.*

BORS:        Bors for England!

*BORS kills LUCAN.*

LANCELOT:    Lancelot

for Guinevere and for pleasure.

*LANCELOT kills BORS, then suddenly kneels before ARTHUR.*

LANCELOT: The fellowship is broken. I am to blame,
my lord, my liege, my friend. I yield to you
your Guinevere, and vow to live a life
consecrated to God.

ARTHUR: I see, yes well,
all's well that ends, well, not so terribly well,
but, boys will be boys eh, swings and roundabouts.

*GUINEVERE kneels too.*

GUIN: My shame is overwhelming. I too
shall live a life of penitence, but not,
I ought to point out, in the same place *he* does. *(LANCELOT.)*

ARTHUR: What a sad end to the story.

*MORDRED stabs ARTHUR in the back.*

MORDRED: Call that sad?
Notice me *now*, do you?

ARTHUR: I say, I'm dying,
killed by an unknown hand.

MORDRED: It was me, it was me!
King Mordred!

LANCELOT: Not any more.

*LANCELOT kills MORDRED from a kneeling position. ARTHUR dying.*

LANCELOT: Still got it.

ARTHUR: Thus I die, and thus all England
perishes with me…

*He dies. LANCELOT and GUINEVERE praying. ELAINE catatonic, the rest dead. LILY and WATERCUP creep back. LILY signs to WATERCUP.*

WATERCUP: <u>That went well</u>.
Oh, what have we done? All right, <u>what have *I* done</u>.

LILY:          Edrycha ar y llun! [14]

WATERCUP:          Oh sure, look at the picture,
a drop of the blue – they're dead, Lily, they're dead!
They drank the red and went into the future
where they *died* – cos that's what happens in the future!
Lancelot's still alive, look, he's praying,
when he opens his eyes he'll kill us! Oh Lily,
I wanted to be a Knight and have a lady,
but I destroyed all England! I'm going to be hanged!
What? Nothing, that's pretty much it. Oh God!
Concentrate, concentrate, yes, the red and the blue,
one counteracts the other, but we're past that,
what's next, I didn't see that…it's a violet drink,
we mix the two…we drink the violet drink,
and…an old man in a pointy hat will come…
and all will be well, the old man in the pointy hat
will save us! Quick, let's mix the two together…

*They mix the last dregs of Red and Blue.* WATERCUP *drinks.* LILY *isn't so sure.*

WATERCUP:     What are you waiting for? My only friend,
I don't – want to be alone with whatever happens.

*LILY sighs and also drinks the Violet Elixir.*

WATERCUP:     We are going to be all right, Lily, I feel it.
I hear something, he's coming, it must be him,
the old man in the pointy hat! We're saved!

*MRS GORMAN, the toilet cleaner, wheels on her trolley and stops it outside the Conveniences. She goes in and out, cleaning, and hangs a timetable outside.*

WATERCUP:     What are you doing. Excuse me, what are you doing?
MRS G.:     Doin' me job.
WATERCUP:          But you – do you know a man
who's old, with a pointy hat?

[14]     Look at the picture!

| | |
|---|---|
| MRS G.: | What's it to you, love. |
| WATERCUP: | I, um, murdered the, well, I accidentally murdered just about everyone here, and I believe a man in a pointy hat will come from nowhere and put it all right! |
| MRS G.: | You do? Not a churchgoer myself, but: free country. |
| WATERCUP: | It isn't a country at all! I ruined it! Can't you do that another time? |
| MRS G.: | This is the time I do it. |
| WATERCUP: | What's that sign? |
| MRS G.: | It tells me I were here. I tick the box to show all's fine and dandy. |
| WATERCUP: | Fine and dandy? Fine and dandy? The king lies dead and it's fine and dandy? |
| MRS G.: | I'm done now, pet. I do my job and you do yours. Goodbye. |

*MRS GORMAN wheels her trolley away. WATERCUP sinks in despair.*

| | |
|---|---|
| WATERCUP: | A toilet cleaner? A toilet cleaner! I want my old man with a pointy hat and I get a toilet cleaner! Oh God… |

*He dissolves. LILY looks on with scorn, fills a cup of water, throws it over him.*

| | |
|---|---|
| WATERCUP: | Plan B. We'll run away. Let's go. Let's go! |
| LILY: | Ni angen clirio'r llanast ma! [15] |
| WATERCUP: | Clear up the mess? That was Plan A. Plan B is running like hell. Lily, Lily, please! |

[15]    We need to clear up this mess!

*LILY won't budge. WATERCUP flees into the forest. LILY sighs and waves goodbye.*
*Enter MERLIN, an old man with a pointy hat. He advances on LILY.*

MERLIN:          Good God…What happened here?
I got here fast as I could – but I'm too late!
Arthur slain, and all his knights, oh Heavens!
The Queen – Lancelot – gone from the earthly sphere!
Catastrophe, oh! Girl, what happened here?
Girl – do you not speak?
Show me! What happened here? <u>There was a lady</u>,
yes, <u>pushing a trolley</u>, what happened next?
<u>She…cleaned the toilets…then she went away</u>.

*MERLIN looks like thunder. He points at the bodies.*

MERLIN:    I mean – WHAT HAPPENED HERE!

*LILY pretends not to have noticed the bodies. She pretends to be startled, then shrugs.*

MERLIN:    Evidently an imbecile. What's this then…

*He finds a red-stained bottle, tastes the dregs.*

MERLIN:    *Tempus Fugit*. In a crude form, very crude.
Some careless spell's been cast. I can restore them,
but a journey lies before them, through the Valley
of Foul Despair, through fires of – oh I say.
*(He sees ELAINE.)* A flibbertigibbet? A will-o'-the-wisp? A beauty…
Young lady, can you tell me your name?

ELAINE:    Pie. No pie.

*MERLIN sees her blue-stained goblet, tastes the dregs.*

MERLIN:          *Tempus Obstinat.*
But like a fool would make it. She needs *that* stuff,
                      *(The Red Elixir.)*
but it has to be brewed properly. Come with me,
we'll pick some forest flowers and pass the time

> in idle chatter, and the somewhat many years
> between us we shall shorten to a moment…

*LILY points at the bodies and signs to MERLIN.*

MERLIN:     What's that? <u>What about them?</u>
            <u>You're old…you have a pointy hat…help them</u>.
            I'm helping this lady first.
LILY:                   Helpa nhw gynta! [16]
MERLIN:     They need more than an antidote. They need
            to seek the Chapel Perilous. The way
            is bleak, the journey long. Hard by a river,
            in the ruins left by Roman infidels,
            there shines a light, a green light, a – what?

*LILY is pointing to the green light on the top of the Chapel. MERLIN ignores her.*

MERLIN:     Not now, I am making a speech. Hard by a river,
            in the ruins left – will you stop that?
            In a wilderness to the north and west, there shines
            a light so green – look I have a pointy hat
            and I'm speaking!
LILY:       Hen ffwl, ma fe reit na! [17]

*MERLIN turns and sees the Chapel.*

MERLIN:     Well. Yes. *That* Chapel Perilous. I knew that.
            Right. To work.
            Barley, fainites, crosses, kings…

*He waves his wand. The BODIES stand, raise their arms, cross their fingers, and troop out to the Chapel, as if entranced.*

THE BODIES:   *Barley, fainites, crosses, kings*
                  *Truce, barsies, screwsies, scrims*
                  *Pax, skinges, creases, creams*
                  *Barley, fainites, crosses, kings*

[16]    Help them first!
[17]    You old fool, it's right there!

MERLIN:     Satisfied?

*MERLIN points to his hat, then leads ELAINE into the forest. A distant howling. WATERCUP appears elsewhere, glancing desperately behind him.*

WATERCUP:     Oh Elaine, what have I done?
I abandoned you, I deserted my dear sister,
I murdered Knights, I slew the King of England,
and something in this wood is trying to kill me!

*Exit, pursued by a fearsome WHITE KNIGHT in full armour, waving its sword and howling. It runs away into the trees. Silence. LILY is left alone.*

LILY:     Bwyta. Yfed. Ugain mined. Cewch bant. [18]


*END OF ACT ONE*

[18]     Eat. Drink. Twenty minutes. Go away.

# ACT TWO

HERALD:
*Here's what you missed*
*If you were being kissed*
*Or doing your Christmas list*
*Or losing money hand-over-fist*
*Or maybe you were just getting pist-*
*Achios from the pistachio-tree*
*But if so, you better listen to me…*
*Watercup is in love with Elaine,*
*Elaine thinks he's a twit*
*So he learned to make Time fast and slow*
*But he made a pig's ear of it*
*So he ran away and there's hell to pay*
*And now there's a mystical man*
*With a towering hat – if you got all that*
*You're a better man than* I *am*

*MERLIN is interrogating LILY. ELAINE, restored, looks on.*

MERLIN:
Let's go over it again. You say your brother
brewed the potions. <u>Yes</u>. From a book? <u>Yes</u>.
So where is this mysterious book? <u>Right there</u>.
Why didn't you just say that the first time?
<u>Nobody was…watching</u>. What does she mean
nobody was watching?

ELAINE:
       Her name's Lily,
she speaks some cuckoo language. She is a simple
country thing, I wish I was just like her,
I mean, I'd still talk normally, I wouldn't
live in the woods like that or wear those clothes,
but otherwise just like her.

MERLIN:
       I would wish you
exactly as you are…

ELAINE:        Please don't wish me
anything, I've heard about your kind.
You and your big stick there.     *(Wand.)*

MERLIN:       I'm sorry? Oh yes.

*MERLIN looks in the Almanack. LUCAN and BORS return to the puppet tent.*

LUCAN:     What are you on about, Sir Bors?

BORS:       I always
think it's interesting to report my dreams
to other people. That way other people
get an insight into my personality.

LUCAN:     I had a dream myself, we were all fighting,
us knights, next thing I knew it were all green
and I were in some church…that's how I knew
I were dreaming, I were in church.

BORS:       In *my* dream –

LUCAN:         We're back,
we're live and we're Lucan for love!

BORS:       And Bors for England.
This Afternoon the Passage-of-Arms will feature
local knights testing themselves in combat
against the cream of Camelot and that cream
will come out fighting.

LUCAN:     It is top-level cream
and we're lapping it up at the Chapel of Sir Groevanor.

MERLIN:    *Tempus Fugit, Tempus Obstinat…*
Mix them together and what…

LILY:        Ma na hen ddyn mewn het bigog
yn dod a bydd popeth yn iawn! [19]

MERLIN:    What's that,
me? this is not me, this is – this is –
oh no. Oh no! Nightmare!

[19]    An old man in a pointy hat comes, and all will be well!

ELAINE:     Do you mean nightmare
            in a negative way?

MERLIN: *(To LILY.)* Did he mix the two together?
            Yes…it was violet. Did he drink the mixture?

LILY:       Yeah a fi. [20]

MERLIN:     A Violet Elixir, no!
            This picture here, this man with a hat, this means
            a figure of the future, this means
            *himself* in the time-to-come – he has both frozen
            himself in youth and conjured himself in age!
            There is *Another* of him in this same forest!

ELAINE:     You mean, another Watercup? That's a good thing,
            isn't it, or it would be if I liked him,
            but I don't so it's terrible news! Oh no!

MERLIN:     And if
            the two should meet, the two come face-to-face…

ELAINE:     Well they'd have a lot in common.

MERLIN:     Oh, poor maiden,
            God save our souls. Observe the final picture:
            the sundial has no dial,
            the clock no hands. Time will stop forever.

ELAINE:     That's bad, isn't it.

MERLIN:     I have to think, *think!*

ELAINE:     I think she's saying she also drank the drink.     *(LILY.)*

*While MERLIN says the following, MRS GORMAN wheels her trolley
on, checks the Conveniences, ticks the grid again and wheels her trolley off.
No one notices.*

MERLIN:     What? That doesn't matter. In old age
            she'd simply be some other forgotten creature,
            some poor neglected dogsbody in shadow,
            it's what *men* do that matters. Forest elf,
            what did your brother want to be in the future?

[20]     Yes, so did I.

*LILY makes the sign of riding and sound of galloping.*

| | |
|---|---|
| ELAINE: | A horse! |
| MERLIN: | A knight! He wanted to be a knight… |
| ELAINE: | That sounded more like a horse, Lily. |
| LUCAN: | Hey, Bors, |
| | you ever seen *him* before? |

*LUCAN and BORS are looking out at the Lists.*

BORS: Well it's not Sir Capenhurst, he's vert-and-argent
on a lozenge, and it's not Sir Balderton,
he's gules-and-sable horizontal, it's not
Sir Cotton Edmunds, he's /usually –

LUCAN: SHUT UP!
I don't want to know who it's not.
I want to know who it is. He's a big lad,
and he seems to be challenging anyone to fight him.

MERLIN: What did you say?

LUCAN: Take a look for yourself, old man.
He just sits there and waits, clad all in white.
They're calling him the Knight With No Name.

*MERLIN looks out at the Lists, beckons LILY to join him. ELAINE comes too.*

MERLIN: Forest elf, come hither. Is that your brother?
He's in…full armour…how the…hell…would *I* know.

ELAINE: It *could* be Watercup, if he were massive
and owned a horse, and we were in the future,
but he isn't, and he doesn't, and we aren't,
are we? I mean, not yet. I suppose we will be.

MERLIN: *(To BORS.)* And you've never seen that knight until this
moment?

BORS: His current average is nought over nought-
point-nought for nought.

MERLIN: What?

LUCAN: No, we've not seen him.
It's like he dropped from the sky. The local knights

have melted away, they don't fancy the challenge. Ladies
are swooning, standing up again, seeing the stranger
and swooning again!

BORS:              The Crusaders of St John's
Ambulance Service have got their work cut out.

LUCAN:         Here comes Mordred, *he's* up for the challenge…

*MERLIN, LILY and ELAINE leave the puppet tent.*

MERLIN:        Tell me about her brother, what does he look like?

ELAINE:        A nobody. When I first saw him, I said
*oh look, there's a nobody there, and –*

MERLIN:                What's *she* saying?

*LILY is signing furiously to MERLIN.*

MERLIN:        <u>He…loves…the stupid lady</u>. He loves you?

ELAINE:        Are you calling me stupid?

MERLIN:                Time could stop forever!
This is not a time to take things personally!

ELAINE:        I might be stupid sometimes, but at least
I don't look a hundred and ten.

MERLIN:                That's quite absurd.
The consensus is I look middle-aged.

LILY:                  Ffwls.
Ma brawd fi'n mynd i dod nol achos
ma fe mewn cariad a fi'n
gwybod be ma fe fel. [21]

MERLIN:                You say he'll come back here?

ELAINE:        He can do as he likes, it won't mean a thing to me.

MERLIN:        Won't mean a thing? Except that Time will cease!
The White Knight *cannot* meet him!

[21]   Fools.
       My brother will come back because
       he's in love, and
       I know what he's like.

| | |
|---|---|
| ELAINE: | Explain again, |
| | *what* has the Knight to do with Watercup? |
| MERLIN: | The Knight *is* Watercup! |
| ELAINE: | No *seriously* |
| | what has the Knight to do with Watercup. |
| MERLIN: | Oh, |
| | *ignoramus!* |
| ELAINE: | Don't cast a spell on me! |
| MERLIN: | I'm *calling* you an ignoramus. |
| ELAINE: | Oh. |
| | Phew. |
| MERLIN: | The Knight was Watercup in the past. |
| | Watercup will *be* the Knight in the future. |
| | Oblivion will follow if they meet. |
| ELAINE: | But why? |
| MERLIN: | What? Because they are – the same! |
| ELAINE: | The same as what? |
| MERLIN: | Each other! The same person! |
| ELAINE: | What's wrong with that? If I met myself-when-young |
| | I'd give myself advice on what to do |
| | when I meet myself-when-old, so when I did |
| | I wouldn't be afraid, I'd thank myself |
| | for my wise words… |
| MERLIN: | Enough! |
| ELAINE: | …I would give myself |
| | a set of bath oils, that's what you give old ladies. |
| MERLIN: | They must *never* meet! |
| ELAINE: | Meet as in shake hands, |
| | or wave across a room? Or simply pass by |
| | at a village fair? How do you *measure* meeting? |
| | And surely if he meets his future self, |
| | then his future self met *him* when he was young |
| | in his past self, but we know the world was fine |
| | because the youth grew old in these same woods |
| | and met a young lad in/ the future – |

MERLIN:             /It's – against the Law!

ELAINE:      The law of what?

MERLIN:                 The Law

             of the Space-Time Continuum.

ELAINE:          The what?

MERLIN:      The Space-Time Continuum.

ELAINE:          The what?

MERLIN:      The Space-Time Continuum.

ELAINE:          The what?

MERLIN:      Continuum.

ELAINE:          The –

MERLIN:                 Continuum. Quantum.

ELAINE:      The what?

MERLIN:             Continuum. Quantum. Quark.

             Quasar.

ELAINE:          But –

MERLIN:                 Continuum.

ELAINE:                 But –

MERLIN: *(Pointing.)*                 Hat.

ELAINE:      But –

MERLIN:          Hat.

ELAINE:             I –

MERLIN:                 Magic.

ELAINE:                    I –

MERLIN:                       Hat.

ELAINE:      Oh. I think I see. What can we do?

MERLIN:      You, nothing. I? I must take steps

             to render a chance collision of the two

             theoretically impossible.

ELAINE:          What does that mean?

MERLIN:      I have to reduce the unstable atomic structure

             to fifty percent of itself.

ELAINE:          What does that mean?

MERLIN:      I have to destroy Watercup.

ELAINE:          Oh no!

Destroy the Knight, not Watercup! I mean,
I *know* Watercup, I mean we're not best friends
but he means no harm.

MERLIN:             Means no harm? He has placed
the Universe on the brink of cataclysm!

ELAINE:     Yes, but he's probably kicking himself, I would be.

MERLIN:     Continuum!

ELAINE:         But –

MERLIN:                 Continuum!

ELAINE:                     But –

MERLIN:                             Hat!

He who stands guilty of this breach in Time
must pay the ultimate price. Watercup
must be destroyed. I shall observe the Lists,
make sure the White Knight stays there. You must watch
for Watercup. If he returns, send word
by the simple creature, then: I shall do
That Which Must Be Done.

*MERLIN goes to the Tournament.*

ELAINE:     Lily, what can we do? Sshh…you're…trying to think.
I'll try to think as well… I like it quiet
when I'm trying to think… It's quiet here, I mean,
apart from someone talking. Oh that's me.
Sshh…that's better. – I think it's really unfair
Watercup has to be destroyed, I *hate*
that stupid Continuing!

LILY:             Edrychwn ni mas amdano fe… [22]

ELAINE:     We'll watch for him…

LILY:                 Os welwn ni fe… [23]

[22]    We'll watch for him...

[23]    If we see him...

217

| ELAINE: | If we see him… |
| LILY: | Rhedwn ni bant dan gilydd… [24] |
| ELAINE: | Run away |

together, yes! No…*we'll* run away together.
*You'll*…run away together. Oh. Yes.
And never…be seen again. Right. Good.
All right. A little bit sad, but…sensible,
in the circumstances, and nothing to do with me,
what Watercup gets up to, running away
or not running away. Better than having Time
and the Universe, like, end.
I suppose. There'd still be a Universe, just not
one where I'll see them again, him and his sister,
one where I call him a nobody or call her
a simple nobody – as if that matters at all!
No one would miss them much. Come on then, Lily,
let's watch at the forest edge. If we never find him,
we'll never see him again, and if we find him,
I'll never see him or you again. What a sad day
it turned to, when it started out so jolly.

*ELAINE and LILY keep watch for WATERCUP. Elsewhere, WATERCUP climbs down
out of a tree in the wood, with a bag.*

WATERCUP:   Did you see him? A huge white knight, I think I lost him,
he was *this* tall, he was breathing fire and his eyes –
Who am I talking to? – My wits are turning
for grief and sorrow, O Elaine, Elaine,
I turned you to a simpleton, and my sister,
poor Lily, you'll be blamed
for the death of Arthur and his gallant knights,
the annihilation of the Realm of England! Oh
why did I ever read that book? The red,
the blue, we are dead, or good as dead – and the violet?

[24]    We'll run away together…

Nothing came at all. No old man
in a pointy hat, no hat, no happy end!
How can I help Elaine or rescue Lily?
I'll be killed if I show my face! And that's why…
out of wolf-hairs, weasel-pelt and egg-yolk…
have I fashioned this impenetrable disguise.

*He produces a rubbish blonde wig from his bag, and puts it on.*

WATERCUP:  I am not Watercup, nor he I was
before I took that name. To the river bank
I went, to muse upon this, and the water
spoke: *You are Dee, Poor Dee, the River-Girl.*
To the Chapel of Sir Groevanor!

*He returns to the Tournament, as the drum-roll signals the afternoon's first Joust.*

LUCAN:  *Now* we'll see what he's made of, this White Giant
who's come from nowhere to lay down his challenge.

BORS:  Mordred's on his horse now, it's a long shot,
it's a funny old game and they're under starter's orders…

*ELAINE and LILY see WATERCUP arrive. So does LUCAN.*

ELAINE:  Who goes there?

LUCAN:  Aye-aye, don't mind if I do.
What's your name, little lady?

BORS:  Lucan, the Lists.

WATERCUP:  I be – Poor Dee, Poor Dee the River-Girl.
I be lost in the forest. (Elaine seems restored –
and the knights are as they were – but I can't risk it,
I'll be burned for witchcraft, hung for poisoning.)

ELAINE: *(To LILY.)* Come with me, Poor Dee, we're on the lookout
for a boy in trouble, but, between ourselves,
I was getting bored of that, Lily can do it,
and you know what I'm in the mood for? Girl-talk!

WATERCUP:  Who is this boy in trouble?

| | |
|---|---|
| ELAINE: | Oh some boy, |
| | he's in trouble but I don't care, I do in a way, |
| | you should always care, I care about him, well I don't, |
| | but I do, in fact – and this is something I'd only |
| | *ever* say to my best friend in the world |
| | and that's you, by the way – deep down, I *quite like him.* |
| WATERCUP: | You *do?* |
| ELAINE: | Oh that's a secret! |
| | Clap hands. Now turn around. Now jump up and down. |
| | Now stand on one leg. Now make a wish. That's good. |
| | The secret is safe. Anyway, he's a nobody, |
| | and I'm destined to marry a Knight. Forget all about him, |
| | cuz, can I call you cuz? |
| WATERCUP: | Er, what's a cuz? |
| ELAINE: | I don't know, but you're *my* cuz! |
| WATERCUP: | Yes, er, cuz, |
| | why is this boy in trouble? |
| ELAINE: | Oh, it's nothing. |
| | I think he's put the Universe in danger. |
| WATERCUP: | He has? |
| ELAINE: | I know, he's so silly! And this ancient |
| | cove in a hat says Time will stop forever. |
| WATERCUP: | *What???* |
| ELAINE: | It's more polite to say *beg your pardon.* |
| | But yes, the world will end, cuz. |
| WATERCUP: | *Oh no!* |
| ELAINE: | It's all very interesting. |
| WATERCUP: | *Oh no! Oh no!* |
| ELAINE: | You're a very good listener, cuz. You and me |
| | are going to be inseparable! Night and day |
| | we shall laze serenely in my leafy bower, |
| | cast off our clothes and talk of love together! |
| WATERCUP: | *(Low.)* Er, very well. |
| ELAINE: | You've a low voice. |
| WATERCUP: | *(High.)* Very well! |

*The trumpet sounds.*

ELAINE: But the Passage-of-Arms is starting, I have a seat,
you'll have to wait for me, cuz!

WATERCUP: I shall wait right here!

*ELAINE rushes out to the Tournament.*

WATERCUP: – She likes me! Time will come to an end but *she likes me!*
I've caused the end of the world but *she quite likes me!*

*WATERCUP drinks some wine he finds, then has to nip to the Knights' toilet.*

BORS: All eyes on the mysterious White Horseman
as he starts his gallop, it's white against black, it's like some
game of chess if chess was played on horseback
with lances in a big field…

LUCAN: And bang!
Mordred's down, that's jousting, done and dusted,
wham-bam-Bedivere!

BORS: I'm Bors for England.

LUCAN: I'm Lucan for Love. The Nameless White Knight
sits tall in his white saddle.

BORS: *Where does he come from?*
*Who is his Lady? What is his name?* Just three
of the questions we'll be asking.

LUCAN: *We don't have*
*the foggiest idea* – that's just one
of the answers you'll get. In fact it's the only one.

*ELAINE returns.*

ELAINE: Who *is* that man? Where does he come from?
How could *he* be Watercup in the future,
past *or* present? The old man is demented.
Watercup is a weed, but the White Knight's
a wonder! Oh, his name must have three parts!
What's Lancelot compared to him? Cuz! Cuz?

*WATERCUP comes out of the Knights'.*

WATERCUP: I'm here, cuz, shall we start
serenely lazing, casting off clothes and so on?
Or you could cast off yours and I could advise you
maybe…

ELAINE: Yes, on what I should wear beneath,
in the silken colours of the new Knight I favour,
and I'd do the same for you.

WATERCUP: There's no *pressing* need
for you to do that, my cuz, I exist to serve you.
So where's that leafy bower you mentioned, I –
what?

ELAINE: You – just – came out of the tent for Knights.
Why?

WATERCUP: Because (good point) in my spare time, cuz,
I work with that woman who ticks the box, you see,
here's me ticking the box. Ticked it. There.

*WATERCUP ticks the box.*

WATERCUP: All clean back there, shipshape, no worries.

ELAINE: Oh, cuz,
we're the best friends in the world, forget all that,
all labour, duty, obligation. Our time
will be slow and soft and sensual, we shall dream
of knights together.

WATERCUP: Nights together…

ELAINE: Bold knights
and bashful knights –

WATERCUP: Oh I see what you mean, yes *knights*,
of course.

ELAINE: Of handsome knights, heroic knights,
mischievous knights and muscular knights, oho!
We shall have gay talk of knights!

WATERCUP: We certainly shall.

ELAINE: Let me tell you about the mysterious White Knight…

*The* HERALD *bring* MORDRED *back, bloody.* LILY *assesses him.*

HERALD:      Water cup!

WATERCUP:          Yes?

ELAINE:                  What do you mean, Yes?

WATERCUP:   Yes, I mean – look, a water cup, right there!
That's a water cup, spot on. Table? Yes!
Picnic basket? Yes!

ELAINE:          You're my funny cuz.
When you said 'water cup' it reminded me
of Watercup. How strange.

LILY *is urgently showing* MORDRED *something from the Almanack.*

MORDRED:       What are you saying?
I should have dipped the lance? What do *you* know, peasant?
Heal my wounds and crawl back in your hole!

WATERCUP *strides across and thumps* MORDRED, *laying him out.*

WATERCUP:   Don't talk to my sister like that!

LILY:         Watercup!!!

ELAINE:         *Watercup*???

LILY *hugs* WATERCUP. ELAINE *watches in astonishment.*

LILY:         Mae'r dyn yn y het bigog ar dy ol di!
Rhed bant! [25]

WATERCUP:      Run away? Run away?
I'm here to atone for everything, to put right
all my wrongs. Sister: heal this man.

LILY *pulls* MORDRED *into the healing tent.* WATERCUP, *heroic, turns to face*
ELAINE – *who thumps him.*

ELAINE:         Watercup, I shall say this only once.

---

[25]    The man in the pointy hat is after you!
Run away!

I am glad that Time will cease and the Universe
end forever, because I shall no longer
be forced to look at your ludicrous silly face.
We shall never meet again, whether the World
end right now or never.

WATERCUP:             What do you mean
*end*? Where's the old man with the pointy hat?

ELAINE:      He's at the jousts. If he finds you he will kill you!
The White Knight's *You-Grown-Up*, I mean, it's not,
that's nonsense actually, as I just watched
the Knight in action and he's not a weed like you,
Watercup, but the mad old bloke does think that,
that if you and the White Knight touch each other, all Time
will cease or something, he has a hat and he says so,
so I'm simply saying, in passing –

WATERCUP:             Stop talking!

ELAINE:      What? I mean *beg your pardon.*

WATERCUP:      There's something I have to tell you.

ELAINE:             Watercup
I've heard enough from you. What is it, though.
You can say what it is, then go away.

WATERCUP:             It's about –
it's about –

ELAINE:             You've no time to waste!
The old man's going to turn you into – dead!

WATERCUP:      I don't care.

ELAINE:             And Time will cease forever!

WATERCUP:      I don't care.

ELAINE:             And the Universe will end!

WATERCUP:      There is something I care *more* about!

ELAINE:             There is?
What?

WATERCUP:             I – I – I –

LILY: Hen ddyn!

Het bigog! Me fe'n dod! [26]

MERLIN: *(From off.)* Dear lady? Lady Elaine?

ELAINE: He can't find you here!

*ELAINE puts the wig back on WATERCUP, as MERLIN arrives.*

ELAINE: Look this is my cuz.

WATERCUP: Hello I'm her cuz.

MERLIN: Comeliness abounding…What is your name?

WATERCUP: Poor Dee, I be, the river-girl.

MERLIN: Pray, how

can one man ever choose when beauty walks

so many-petalled?

LUCAN: And here comes Gawain,

and ouch, there goes Gawain.

BORS: Gawain is down,

and the White Knight is ploughing a great white furrow

through Camelot!

LUCAN: There's Lancelot, he'll stop this,

for the honour of King Arthur!

BORS: For England!

MERLIN: Is there any sign of the boy?

ELAINE: No sign at all.

Did you see a boy, Poor Dee? No, you didn't,

did you, you're a girl.

WATERCUP: What has this boy

done wrong, venerable sir?

MERLIN: He has jeopardised

the Universe!

WATERCUP: I'm sure he didn't mean to.

ELAINE: I'll explain it later, cuz, it's about the Quango

Continuing in Time and Space or something.

[26] Old man!

Pointy hat! He's coming!

*The HERALD brings GAWAIN back, bloody and dazed.*

| | |
|---|---|
| HERALD: | Watercup! |
| GAWAIN: | Donald…where's yer trewsers… |
| HERALD: | Watercup? WATERCUP! |
| WATERCUP: | LILY! |

*LILY comes out with the healed MORDRED, brings the wounded GAWAIN in.*

MERLIN:         Why did she just say *Lily*?

ELAINE:               It's what she calls me.
Don't you, Dee.

WATERCUP:               Yes, Elaine. I mean Lily. Lily!

LUCAN:         And here comes Lancelot on Boy Legend,
Lancelot of the Lake, pride of England!

BORS:         He'll have to restore some pride, for this White Knight
has made a mockery of the form-book.

MERLIN:               Pray
the White Knight is victorious. If he's wounded
he'll come this way and all my instincts tell me
Watercup is close by.

LUCAN:               Here they come
and bang, it's over, good-night folks, and good-night
Lancelot! Amazing!

BORS:               The White Knight
has vanquished every Knight of Camelot!

MERLIN:         Is he riding away? Is the White Knight riding away?

LUCAN:         No he's sat there on his horse. It's like he's waiting…

*LILY brings the restored GAWAIN out and is showing him the Almanack.*

GAWAIN:         <u>So I…wore my shield too high…</u> Mebbe you're right.
Och I'm too old for this, I'm getting coached
by a wee lassie, I'm out.

*GAWAIN joins LUCAN and BORS.*

ELAINE:         Cuz, Poor Dee, what did you want to tell me?

WATERCUP: Nothing, cuz, except that in the forest
I *met* a boy in trouble. He said that one day
the world would see him fight in a noble cause
against impossible odds, and for a lady.

ELAINE: Did he say who that lady was?

WATERCUP: He was about to,
when –

*The HERALD comes back with the only slightly wounded LANCELOT.*

HERALD: Water cup!

LANCELOT: Thanks, old bean, I can manage.

*(To ELAINE.)* Hey little poetry lady, I've a news-flash.
That Dum-de-dum of yours is back in business!

*LILY escorts LANCELOT into the healing tent. ARTHUR and GUINEVERE arrive.*

ARTHUR: Anyone seen my Knights at all? No rush,
but a giant Foe is out there on his giant, you know,
horse, and there's no one left.

GUIN: That's because your Knights
are alcoholic good-for-nothing pillocks
who haven't fought a battle since the Romans
took their toys away.

MERLIN: Arthur, hear me,
the peril is far graver than you know!

ARTHUR: Where the deuce have *you* been? You always
come when it's too late.

MERLIN: I was in the forest,
gathering my thoughts.

GUIN: Oh that's useful,
shall I make them into soup?

ARTHUR: Sir Lancelot?
Sir Gawain? Sir Mordred?

*The KNIGHTS emerge. LILY is showing LANCELOT the Almanack.*

LANCELOT: So you think I should take my head out of my – I say, it's all gone quiet.

ARTHUR:          Knights of Camelot,
would you mind awfully taking another crack
at the gentleman on the horse? Mordred, old chap?

MORDRED:   I hereby announce my retirement from jousting,
your so-called Majesty. From this day on
I shall report on sport for the small people
who can't see over the crowd. Ninety-nine jousts.
Ninety-eight defeats. I'll always have Lincoln.

*MORDRED sticks his sword in the ground and goes to the puppet tent.*

ARTHUR:    Gawain? Will you not challenge the White Horseman?

GAWAIN:    Make way for an old dog there, the game's moved on,
I've not a clue what I'm doin', I'll be an expert.

*GAWAIN sticks his sword in the ground and goes to the puppet tent.*

ARTHUR:    Lancelot? Champion?

LANCELOT:       Well, the thing of it is,
I had a good innings, eh, perhaps this chap
is the new me, so to speak. Best of British,
Sir Dum-de-dum! Is there any prosecco going?

*LANCELOT sticks his sword in the ground and goes to the puppet tent.*

GUIN:    *(To ARTHUR.)* Don't look at me like that. It's your gang.
Somebody pour me a double and I'll drink
to losers I have loved.

*GUINEVERE joins the KNIGHTS in the puppet tent.*

ARTHUR:        Well. I say.
So passes the, you know,
glory that was – well, was glorious.
I don't have a speech prepared. Where's that Herald?
He could sing about, you know, sweet things ending,
make it not seem so bad. *Heigh-ho*, it could go,
in the chorus, *heigh-ho, heigh-ho, heigh-ho* oh heck.

*The* WHITE KNIGHT *comes, haughty, mysterious, faceless, sword raised. The* KNIGHTS *cower. The* WHITE KNIGHT *advances on* ARTHUR.

ARTHUR:     I suppose *I* have to fight him, which is, well,
            not how I planned to bid ye goodbye. As I say,
            I don't have a speech prepared. Perhaps you could say
            my last day was my favourite day, and it was.
            In fact it always was, now I think about it.
            Well, here goes. For England. *Heigh-ho.*

WATERCUP *steps forth, throws off his wig, pulls Lancelot's sword from the ground.*

WATERCUP:   Sheathe your sword, your Highness, *I* shall fight him!
            For the Lady of The Woods!
ELAINE:              Watercup, no!
LILY:       Ma hyn yn dwp, hyn yn oed i ti. [27]
MERLIN:     *Watercup? No!* It cannot be!
            This boy and this mysterious White Knight
            are the same person, sundered by the years,
            but drawn together in this place by witchcraft!
            Were they to touch, then all the Universe
            would crumble, and Time cease!

*Everyone goes still.*

MERLIN:              – I am too late.
            It is done. And so begins…
            The Age of Oblivion.
ARTHUR:     Sorry, old chap, I think we were all a bit shocked
            at the crap you just came out with.
WATERCUP:            Time, cease!
            Universe, crumble to dust! I have no fear.
            I am Watercup of the Weeds, your Majesty,
            and I will fight this brute to restore the honour
            of Camelot.

[27]    This is stupid, even for you.

MERLIN:          This cannot be!

ARTHUR:          Knights,

restrain the old boy, will you, senior moment.

Watercup of the Weeds, I salute you.

Should you triumph, I mean in theory should you triumph,

can't quite see it myself but I *am* a fan,

so in the unlikely event you be not slaughtered,

savaged, dismembered or decapitated,

what do you ask in return?

WATERCUP:      What do I ask?

I ask to be admitted to the ranks

of the Legendary Knights of Camelot,

as *Sir* Watercup, so that the Lady Elaine

might find me worthy of her hand in marriage.

ELAINE:        Oh! I'm going to swoon – but I'll miss something!

You like me! You quite like me!

WATERCUP:      I quite love you.

'One day you shall see me fight in a noble cause

against impossible odds, and for a lady.'

ELAINE:        But I thought you were a halfwit then! Now you love me

and you're going to go and die!

MERLIN:          All will die!

There'll be no such thing as *anything*!

ARTHUR:         Pipe down,

old boy, pipe down. *Heigh-ho* all you subjects,

young Watercup will fight. If he prevails

I shall make a Knight of him!

Let Time cease and the Universe crumble, England

loves an underdog!

*The WHITE KNIGHT and WATERCUP fight. WATERCUP falls, and the WHITE KNIGHT
stands over him, sword-point to his neck. No one can look, then suddenly.*

*ELAINE runs up and kneels beneath the sword.*

ELAINE: White Knight, stranger, enemy of all
I know, please take my life – but only spare
the life of the boy I love!

*The WHITE KNIGHT seems to ponder awhile. Then he sticks his sword in the ground with the other swords, and extends his hand to the fallen WATERCUP.*

MERLIN: I tell you – Time will cease!

*WATERCUP and the WHITE KNIGHT clasp hands, and the KNIGHT lifts WATERCUP to his feet. WATERCUP and ELAINE embrace.*

ARTHUR: I don't know if Time ceased or not, old man,
but that was a corking gesture from the fellow,
not to mention the lady. Watercup,
for your courage in the face of quite absurd
and faintly embarrassing odds, I do dub thee
Sir Watercup of the Weeds. O White Knight
who has given all of Camelot a lesson
in arms and in good grace, will you not reveal
your name and origins?

*The WHITE KNIGHT seems to stare at ARTHUR. Then he starts to make signs, and WATERCUP finds he can understand them.*

WATERCUP: <u>...I...don't know where I come from...I was walking</u>
<u>in the forest, I was afraid, I cried out...</u>
<u>then I saw your men on horseback...I always</u>
<u>loved the jousting...when I was...a little...</u>
<u>girl... I used to go to the tournaments</u>
<u>and heal the fallen knights...one day my brother</u>
<u>found an old book...and that day I decided</u>
<u>to make myself...so big and strong...that one day</u>
<u>I could fight the noblest champions of the kingdom...</u>

*The WHITE KNIGHT notices LILY doing the same signs as she is. They move towards each other, but MERLIN thrusts himself between them.*

MERLIN: I tell you, Time will cease! You cannot touch her!
WATERCUP: Time didn't cease when she shook me by the hand.

MERLIN: But the White Knight isn't Watercup – she's *her!*

ARTHUR: Then who the deuce did Watercup become?

*MRS GORMAN wheels her trolley into the scene.*

ELAINE: Watercup, you became a toilet cleaner,
and a woman, that's disappointing on every level.

MERLIN: Do you have to do that now?

MRS G.: Wonder of wonders,
Merlin...

WATERCUP: Merlin?

MRS G.: You noticed me! 'Just some forgotten creature,
some poor neglected dogsbody in shadow.
For it's what *men* do that matters.'

*MRS GORMAN throws off her overalls and reveals herself to be MORGANA.*

MORGANA: Do you remember, Merlin?

MERLIN: Morgana...
Worst nightmare! Nemesis!

ARTHUR: Here we go again.

MERLIN: Spawn of the Devil!

MORGANA: Merlin, calm down, dear,
I'm someone just like you. Except I'm slightly
better than you at magic.

MERLIN: That's what I mean –
my worst nightmare! You used to look like – that!
At the Academy –

MORGANA: I used to look like this.

MERLIN: But you *can't* – it was, it was centuries ago!

MORGANA: We were partners there, in the potion-room, remember?
You would stir your chemicals and cast your spells
then, when the dust had settled on your usual
wreck of smoking ruins and aberrations,
I was left to mop things up. I did so gladly,
Merlin, I'm doing it now.

WATERCUP: What did you call him?

MORGANA:  *(To MERLIN.)* Why are you always late? Why do you always
miss the start of the day?

MERLIN:  I was – in the forest –

MORGANA:  You find yourself in the forest.

MERLIN:  On the path,
in sunlight, patterned sunlight…

MORGANA:  Are you a child there,
a young man or an old?

MERLIN:  I am – all three.
I was – thinking about the world,
how – marvellous it was, but all the while
how evil lurked behind the trees…I wished
to learn, to make the world a better place…
I thought I might find answers – in a book.

MORGANA:  Was that once upon a time? Or on this day?

WATERCUP:  *(To MORGANA.)* Why do you – call him Merlin? That's my –

MERLIN: *(To WATERCUP.)*  Don't touch me!

MORGANA:  Oh Merlin, Merlin, Time stopped long ago.
No harm can come where we are. Take his hand.
*(To MERLIN and WATERCUP.)* It's your own hand, won't you take it?

MERLIN:  This fool was never me.

WATERCUP:  I'll never be
a fool like that!

MERLIN:  I was the brightest boy
in the Academy!

MORGANA:  You were the only boy.
Behind the nine bright girls.

WATERCUP:  He can't be me!
I've just been made a Knight, and look at him!

MERLIN:  Look at *me*? Look at *me*? Give him ten minutes
with a library book and he makes the bloody world end!
Call yourself a wizard?

WATERCUP:  Old fool,
I call myself Sir Watercup of the Weeds!

MERLIN:  *And* he gets the girl – how is *that* fair?

Why don't I remember her? Why don't I remember
*him?*

MORGANA: *(To MERLIN and WATERCUP.)* Merlin, Merlin, one day
you start at the Academy, one day
you never went at all. One day you find
a girl on the forest path and fall in love.
One day you creep on either side of hedges,
Merlin and Elaine,
and perhaps you hear a crackle underfoot
but think no more of it, and go your ways
and never meet in this world. All your days
begin on the forest path,
and here they end. They leave no consequences,
no effects, except, in waking dreams
at times you recollect those other lives
and wonder what they were. Some day this sword
is hard to pull from here, it takes a nobody.

ARTHUR: I say, that *is* a dream I had.

MORGANA: Some day
a picnic blanket is a Round Table.

LANCELOT: Blimey,
Guin, are you following this?

GUIN: She talks a lot
for a toilet cleaner.

MORGANA: Some day even a humble
water cup is holy, and these men
give half their lives to find it. But today
this was the life you chose. This was the day
a boy tried out some magic.

MERLIN/WATERCUP: But I –

MORGANA: Merlin:
we nine bright girls all wear this golden crystal:
here all your days are kept.

MERLIN/WATERCUP: But he –

MORGANA: Merlin:

234

*(Pointing.)* Crystal.

MERLIN/WATERCUP:  But I –

MORGANA:  Magic.

MERLIN/WATERCUP:  How can –

MORGANA:  Crystal.

We threw a ring around you all, a circle
to save you for all time, to pass your days
and tell your tales. From time to time we visit,
disguised as those whom you would take for granted.
In coats and hats we watch you from the future.
We ascertain there is no breach or gap
by which you might escape the enchanted O
and suffer the world out there.
Over that line, beyond the woods – is Time,
loss, sickness, death. All creatures there they merely
come and go, just once, and not again.
But you are immortal here, in a web of story.
I've ticked the boxes and my work is done.
Tomorrow morning all will begin again.
You will forget what's happened, you'll be strangers
encountered on a forest path, each day
a different outcome. Knights of Camelot,
drink and be glad, life is unending story.

*All Camelot celebrates.* LILY *and the* WHITE KNIGHT *murmur together in Welsh.*

ELAINE:  It will all begin again?

WATERCUP:  I don't want that,
Elaine, I don't *want* a different outcome
every day.

ELAINE:  I don't want to forget
everything, I don't want to forget
anything!

235

| | |
|---|---|
| WATERCUP: | I want the day we've had, a world where this has happened and only this! |
| ELAINE: | A day that has a night! |
| WATERCUP: | A night that has a morning! |
| ELAINE: | A morning with you there! |
| WATERCUP: | Another day we spent until it turned to a yesterday we shared! |
| ELAINE: | What can we do? |
| WATERCUP: | We'll go, we'll run away! |
| ELAINE: | What about Lily? |
| WATERCUP: | She's found another Lily. She's happy. She doesn't need me now. It's now or never. Nobody's watching. We're going to leave these woods, they must end somewhere. That's how far we're going. |

*They kiss, and creep away. ARTHUR signals for the WHITE KNIGHT to kneel.*

| | |
|---|---|
| ARTHUR: | Well I don't understand a word, so no change there! White Horseman, I do dub thee – any ideas? |
| LILY: | Lily. |
| ARTHUR: | Yes, Sir Lily, Sir Lily of what, though? |

*LILY points in the direction of Wales.*

| | |
|---|---|
| LILY: | Galwa fe'n Sir Lily o Gymru. [28] |
| ARTHUR: | What's she pointing at? Ah. I do dub thee Sir Lily of Those Hedges Over There. |
| LANCELOT: | Sir Lily of Those Hedges Over There, I'll see you in the Lists! |
| GAWAIN: | I'll have a crack at ye, too, ye big girl's blouse. |
| MORDRED: | I swear to you, I will fall from my horse one day, but so will you. |

---

[28]    Call him Sir Lily of Wales.

BORS:                That's jousting in a nutshell.

LUCAN:              Wham-bam-Bedivere, goodnight and thank you.

*The KNIGHTS drink. MERLIN sees LILY and the WHITE KNIGHT together.*

MORGANA:      Merlin, what's the matter?

MERLIN:           It's those two.
                    Same-sex relationships, all very well,
                    but that's a same-*person* partnership. I know
                    the Universe won't come to an end, but really,
                    you have to draw the line.

MORGANA:          I spoke at length
                    with my mother, the Ancient Sybil of the Mountains,
                    and she says that love is love between two persons,
                    or, sometimes, between one. Thus spoke the Sybil.

MERLIN:           So you're saying they've got a Sybil partnership.

MORGANA:      My dear, eternity's not time enough
                    for me to find that funny.

*MERLIN notices WATERCUP has gone.*

MERLIN:           Where am I?

MORGANA:          In the woods.

MERLIN:                   No I mean, where am I
                    *young*? And where's my lady?

*All notice WATERCUP and ELAINE are missing.*

MORGANA:          I – don't know –

MERLIN:           Why would they run away? It's a happy ending.

MORGANA:      They won't get very far. As they approach
                    the edges of the wood their memories
                    will start to fail. They won't know one another.

ARTHUR:          Search party! Off we go! Spread out, eh!

*All fan out into the woods. WATERCUP and ELAINE elsewhere.*

ELAINE:            I think we were here before.

WATERCUP:       No I don't think so.

ELAINE:            We were following the sunset.

WATERCUP:              No, no,
                       we were seeking a Tournament.

ELAINE:                I don't think so,
                       Waterlily.

WATERCUP:              Watercup.

ELAINE:                            What's that?

WATERCUP:    I don't know, I was telling you my name,
             Eleanor.

ELAINE:                Emily. No, Allie. Annie.

WATERCUP:    It doesn't matter.

ELAINE:                What doesn't matter?

WATERCUP:                  Our names,
                       they don't matter. We'll hold hands.

ELAINE:                Yes, hold hands.
                       Let's take it in turns to try and remember things.
                       I'll go first.

WATERCUP:              First at what.

ELAINE:                            I don't know.
                       Just hold my hand.

WATERCUP:              I'm holding your hand, Eileen.

ELAINE:      What did you just call me?

WATERCUP:              El – *Elaine!*

ELAINE:      *Water – cup*, let's go this way, quickly,
             things are coming back to me! I'm remembering
             everything!

WATERCUP:              It's coming back,
                       the Tournament, the Book, my sister Lily –
                       I can see the edge of the woods, I can see a light!

*A bright light shines on them.*

ELAINE:      There's a way out of the woods!

WATERCUP:              The toilet cleaner –
                       Morgana, she said she always ticks the boxes,
                       but *I ticked one of them* – she must have thought
                       *she'd* done it! There's a gap we can get out through!

| | |
|---|---|
| ELAINE: | Watercup… |
| WATERCUP: | Elaine? |
| ELAINE: | If we stayed here, all would – begin again. |
| WATERCUP: | What do you mean? |
| ELAINE: | Here, in the woods, it would all *begin*. It would never – end. If we leave the woods, she said, out there – things – will end some day. Us. You and I. All things. |
| WATERCUP: | You think – you think we should turn back? Forget it all? Begin the day again? Pass on either side of hedges… |
| ELAINE: | Hear the crackle underfoot… |
| WATERCUP: | And think no more of it… |
| ELAINE: | And go our ways… |
| WATERCUP: | And never meet in this world. |
| ELAINE: | And you'd be a nobody again and not *my* nobody… |
| WATERCUP: | And there we would stay, forever… |
| ELAINE: | Forever telling different stories… Out there – what if there *are* no stories? Only Time, and loss and death and whatever the other one was. |
| WATERCUP: | What's *that* – compared to *this*? Us, forever! Till it's over. |
| ELAINE: | Us, forever, till it's over. |
| WATERCUP: | Here's my hand. |
| ELAINE: | Here's mine, Sir Watercup of the Weeds. Let's go where things will end some day. Let's go there now, together. |

*ELAINE and WATERCUP run off into the light. The HERALD comes by, and sings.*

HERALD:
*The Seventh of June and the Eighth of May*
*Are happy together a mile away,*
*The Second of March and the Twelfth of July*
*Married in secret and I know why,*
*The Ninth of November will always remember*
*The day she set eyes on the Sixth of September*
　　　*And all that's to be*
　　　*And all that are gone*
*Are off to the dance with their glad-rags on*

*The night you arrive and the day we part*
*Are watching the road from the back of the cart*
*The moment you loved and the hour you lost*
*Are crossing a garden that has to be crossed*
*The year you were fine and the year you were mine*
*Are dining together where we used to dine*
　　　*And all that are gone*
　　　*And all that's to be*
*Is off to the dance with my baby and me*

*ARTHUR, GUINEVERE, MERLIN, MORGANA, LANCELOT, GAWAIN, MORDRED, LUCAN, BORS, THE WHITE KNIGHT and LILY dance.*

　　　*And all that's to come*
　　　*And all that are gone*
*Are off to the dance with their glad-rags on*

*WATERCUP and ELAINE, dressed like people dress today, dance with them all.*

　　　*All that are gone*
　　　*And all that's to be*
*Is off to the dance with my baby and me*

*And all bow, and all dance away.*

\*　　　\*　　　\*　　　\*　　　\*

# WWW.OBERONBOOKS.COM

Follow us on www.twitter.com/@oberonbooks
& www.facebook.com/OberonBooksLondon